▶ **Religious Liberties for Corporations?**

DOI: 10.1057/9781137479709.0001

Other Palgrave Pivot titles

Larner Samuel: Forensic Authorship Analysis and the World Wide Web

Karen Rich: Interviewing Rape Victims: Practice and Policy Issues in an International Context

Vieten M. Ulrike (editor): Revisiting Iris Marionyoung on Normalisation, Inclusion and Democracy

Fuchaka Waswa, Christine Ruth Saru Kilalo, and Dominic Mwambi Mwasaru: Sustainable Community Development: Dilemma of Options in Kenya

Giovanni Barone Adesi: Simulating Security Returns: A Filtered Historical Simulation Approach

Daniel Briggs and Dorina Dobre: Culture and Immigration in Context: An Ethnography of Romanian Migrant Workers in London

M.J. Toswell: Borges the Unacknowledged Medievalist

Anthony Lack: Martin Heidegger on Technology, Ecology, and the Arts

Carlos A. Scolari, Paolo Bertetti and Matthew Freeman: Transmedia Archaeology: Storytelling in the Borderlines of Science Fiction, Comics and Pulp Magazines

Judy Rohrer: Queering the Biopolitics of Citizenship in the Age of Obama

Paul Jackson and Anton Shekhovtsov: The Post-War Anglo-American Far Right: A Special Relationship of Hate

Elliot D. Cohen: Technology of Oppression: Preserving Freedom and Dignity in an Age of Mass, Warrantless Surveillance

Ilan Alon (editor): Social Franchising

Richard Michael O'Meara: Governing Military Technologies in the 21st Century: Ethics and Operations

Thomas Birtchnell and William Hoyle: 3D Printing for Development in the Global South: The 3D4D Challenge

David Fitzgerald and David Ryan: Obama, US Foreign Policy and the Dilemmas of Intervention

Lars Elleström: Media Transformation: The Transfer of Media Characteristics Among Media

Claudio Povolo: The Novelist and the Archivist: Fiction and History in Alessandro Manzoni's The Betrothed

Gerbrand Tholen: The Changing Nature of the Graduate Labour Market: Media, Policy and Political Discourses in the UK

Aaron Stoller: Knowing and Learning as Creative Action: A Reexamination of the Epistemological Foundations of Education

palgrave▸pivot

Religious Liberties for Corporations?: Hobby Lobby, the Affordable Care Act, and the Constitution

David H. Gans
Director of the Human Rights, Civil Rights, and Citizenship Program, Constitutional Accountability Center

and

Ilya Shapiro
Senior Fellow in Constitutional Studies, Cato Institute

With an introduction by Jeffrey Rosen, President of the National Constitution Center

palgrave
macmillan

First published in 2014 by
PALGRAVE MACMILLAN®
in the United States—a division of St. Martin's Press LLC,
175 Fifth Avenue, New York, NY 10010.

Where this book is distributed in the UK, Europe and the rest of the world,
this is by Palgrave Macmillan, a division of Macmillan Publishers Limited,
registered in England, company number 785998, of Houndmills,
Basingstoke, Hampshire RG21 6XS.

Palgrave Macmillan is the global academic imprint of the above companies
and has companies and representatives throughout the world.

Palgrave® and Macmillan® are registered trademarks in the United States,
the United Kingdom, Europe and other countries.

ISBN: 978-1-137-47972-3 EPUB
ISBN: 978-1-137-47970-9 PDF
ISBN: 978-1-137-48467-3 Hardback

Library of Congress Cataloging-in-Publication Data is available from
the Library of Congress.

A catalogue record of the book is available from the British Library.

First edition: 2014

www.palgrave.com/pivot

DOI: 10.1057/9781137479709

Contents

Acknowledgments

This book, which grew out of a series of debates held under the auspices of the National Constitution Center, would not be possible without the efforts of Jeffrey Rosen, Scott Bomboy and the rest of the National Constitution Center team. Special thanks go to Brian O'Connor from Palgrave Macmillan, who encouraged us to take our debates and transform them into a book. Jonathan Blanks, Jack Bussell, Olivia Grady, and Carolyn Iodice provided tremendous assistance in transcribing these debates. For innumerable discussions over the issues raised by the *Hobby Lobby* case, David thanks Douglas Kendall, Elizabeth Wydra, Judith Schaeffer, Brianne Gorod, and Tom Donnelly; Ilya thanks Roger Pilon, Eugene Volokh, Richard Epstein, and Trevor Burrus for the same reason, as well as Kevin Baine, C.J. Mahoney, and Eli Savit for their work on Cato's Supreme Court brief in the case.

DOI: 10.1057/9781137479709.0002

Introduction by Jeffrey Rosen

Abstract: *Jeffrey Rosen, president of the National Constitution Center, explains the role of the NCC in our nation's constitutional discourse. He then introduces the Gans-Shapiro debate over corporate rights, religious liberty, and* Hobby Lobby *and how it originated as a series of NCC podcasts and forums.*

Keywords: Hobby Lobby; National Constitution Center; podcast; We the People

Gans, David H., and Ilya Shapiro. *Religious Liberties for Corporations?: Hobby Lobby, the Affordable Care Act, and the Constitution*. New York: Palgrave Macmillan, 2014. DOI: 10.1057/9781137479709.0003.

I'm Jeffrey Rosen, President and CEO of the National Constitution Center, and it's a pleasure to welcome you to the first book based on our "We The People" Constitutional Podcasts. The National Constitution Center is the only institution in America chartered by Congress "to disseminate information about the U.S. Constitution on a non-partisan basis." Soon after I started here in June, 2013, I decided that the Constitution Center should be the one place in America where citizens can hear all sides on the constitutional debates at the center of our American life so that they can make up their own minds.

Our "We The People" Podcast series is the most direct expression of our aspiration to be America's Town Hall. Every week, my colleagues and I call the leading conservative, liberal, libertarian, or progressive constitutional scholars in America to debate the constitutional issue of the week. These podcasts have been building a national audience, and I've been thrilled by the responsiveness of citizens to substantive constitutional arguments, presented with intelligence and nuance.

One of our earliest podcasts covered *Burwell v. Hobby* Lobby, one of the most hotly contested cases of the Supreme Court's 2013 Term. *Hobby Lobby* (and its companion case, *Conestoga Wood v. Burwell*) raised the question, whether for-profit corporations owned and operated by religiously devout people could claim exemptions from a regulation that implemented the federal Affordable Care Act by requiring employers to provide contraceptive coverage for their employees. We asked David Gans of the Constitutional Accountability Center and Ilya Shapiro of the Cato Institute to discuss whether the rights of corporations differ from those held by natural persons and how that question affects the religious liberty issues at the heart of this case. David and Ilya graciously agreed to be among our first guests on "We The People" podcast series. Their first podcast for us was actually on a different subject, the *McCutcheon* campaign finance case, but their dialogue there was so informative that we invited them to visit us and debate *Hobby Lobby* at a special forum. After posting a recording of that forum online, we asked David and Ilya to return for further analysis after oral argument in the case, and again once the Supreme Court reached its decision. Their trilogy of discussions on corporate rights and religious liberties were instantly popular; the three podcasts were downloaded more than 83,000 times from our website, blog, and iTunes.

David and Ilya's conversations are a wonderful cross between a Charlie Rose-style discussion and the kind of constitutional debate you might

DOI: 10.1057/9781137479709.0003

hear at a law school faculty lunch. Their ability to make the arguments on both sides of the religious liberties debate, calmly but precisely, is a perfect match with our Center's core mission: to provide a nonpartisan venue where ideas can be discussed in constitutional and legal rather than political terms, and where arguments on all sides of the debate can be treated with respect.

David and Ilya's first public discussion took place at a public event as the Constitution Center was hit by an early winter snowstorm. It was one of the most inspiring experiences I had as the new head of the Center, as hardy Philadelphians braved the storm to experience a vigorous constitutional debate.

The program was so impressive because it showed how eager our audience was to understanding the complex issues that David and Ilya set out to debate. Do for-profit corporations have religious rights? Does the Department of Health and Human Services regulation that interprets the Affordable Care Act as requiring these corporations to provide contraceptive coverage violate the First Amendment or the Religious Freedom Restoration Act? And what are the consequences of allowing religious exemptions from generally applicable laws in this context?

What you'll find in the following book are the answers to these questions, in the form of a spirited discussion between two good friends who don't agree on some of the key constitutional and legal issues—but recognize they can learn from each other during the process.

David is the director of the Human Rights, Civil Rights, and Citizenship Program at the Constitutional Accountability Center. He is the author of numerous scholarly works on the Constitution's text and history, including of CAC's Text and History Narrative Series. David regularly participates in Supreme Court litigation. He joined CAC after serving as program director of Cardozo Law School's Floersheimer Center for Constitutional Democracy, and as an attorney with the Brennan Center for Justice at NYU School of Law.

Ilya is a senior fellow in constitutional studies at the Cato Institute and editor-in-chief of the *Cato Supreme Court Review*. He contributes to a variety of academic, popular, and professional publications and regularly provides media commentary, including an appearance on *The Colbert Report*. Ilya has provided testimony to Congress and state legislatures and has filed more than 100 "friend of the court" briefs in the Supreme Court. Before joining Cato, Ilya was a special assistant/advisor to the Multi-National Force in Iraq and litigated at two large law firms.

DOI: 10.1057/9781137479709.0003

Both David and Ilya have a thorough understanding of constitutional history, and their discussions always include thoughtful efforts to relate Founding-era debates to current constitutional questions.

In chapters 1 and 2 of this book, they discuss the rights of corporations, and the issue of corporate personhood and religious liberty: the core subjects of the *Hobby Lobby* ruling.

For example, David argues that "the text, history, and purpose of the constitutional guarantee of the free exercise of religion all make clear that secular, for-profit corporations cannot claim to exercise religion."

Ilya counters that "whatever rights corporations have, whether in the religious area, in political speech, or anything else, aren't due to their being legal persons. They derive instead from the rights of the natural persons of which they are composed."

Another important area where Ilya and David agree to disagree is on the merits of the Religious Freedom Restoration Act (RFRA) after the *Hobby Lobby* and *Conestoga Wood* cases were argued in front on the nine justices.

Chapter 3 of this book comes from a podcast devoted to the questions of RFRA and the broader implications of *Hobby Lobby*. David and Ilya looked at the "slippery slope" that seemed to appear after the arguments, when it became apparent that the justices were less interested in the issue of corporate rights and more focused on the possible consequences of ruling for the plaintiffs' religious liberty claims, and whether that ruling would be broad or narrow.

David argued that it would be unprecedented for the Court to recognize a religious exemption in this context, while Ilya thought that RFRA made the case simpler than most think. They both identified Justice Anthony Kennedy as a key player and discussed how he was likely to view the possible third-party effects of a ruling for *Hobby Lobby*.

Chapter 4 was the concluding program in the series. In a podcast recorded right after the *Hobby Lobby* decision came down, Ilya saw the 5–4 decision as a limited one. He argued that the decision was a correct application of RFRA's statutory language, and a victory for religious liberty, but it wasn't a path-breaking Supreme Court precedent.

"More broadly, this ruling properly limits the power of government to impose these incredible, unprecedented mandates and other types of Leviathan burdens on the citizenry as this administration has. That's why, ultimately, the Court has to make these calls, and adjudicate what, in its time, was the noncontroversial Religious Freedom Restoration Act,

DOI: 10.1057/9781137479709.0003

which was pushed by those religious zealots Ted Kennedy and Chuck Schumer," Ilya concluded, with a wink.

David disagreed. For the first time, he argued, the Court had recognized a corporate right to religious exercise—at the cost of women for whom it will be more difficult to obtain certain contraceptives.

"It creates a very dangerous precedent that threatens to undermine—not protect—religious liberty by exalting the rights of corporations over those individuals who employed there," David concluded. "Under Justice Alito's ruling, if you go to work for Hobby Lobby, your rights are subject to the whims of the owners and can be overridden if the owner insists that your rights conflict with the owner's religious view. That a huge and dangerous change in the law. It gives corporations new rights they never before possessed."

The debate over the First Amendment and corporate religious rights will continue as the Supreme Court faces more decision related to similar issues. And the National Constitution Center will continue to host podcasts on these and other constitutional questions that come before the Court. I'm proud that this book is the first to emerge from our podcast series and look forward to publishing many more. Most of all, I hope you find David and Ilya's discussion of the competing constitutional and legal arguments illuminating, as you make up your own minds about one of the most challenging constitutional and legal questions of our time.

Let me sign off by asking you, as I do at the end of every podcast, to join us for our next "We The People" Constitutional podcasts. On behalf of the National Constitution Center, I'm Jeffrey Rosen.

Philadelphia, August 2014

DOI: 10.1057/9781137479709.0003

1

What Rights Do Corporations Have?

Abstract: This chapter examines the idea of corporate personhood and the rights that flow from it. Gans argues that the Constitution never mentions corporations and doesn't give corporations the same rights as individuals. He asserts that the Founders understood that there were fundamental differences between individuals and corporations, which received special privileges that individuals didn't. While corporations have some rights, he argues that the Constitution cannot be applied wholesale to them. Shapiro agrees that corporations—or other groups of people, regardless of legal form—don't have the same rights as humans. He gives several examples of corporate rights, however, and concludes that they're a subset of the rights of natural persons. The disagreement here is over the scope of those rights and how to apply them.

Keywords: Citizens United; constitutional text and history; corporate personhood; corporate rights; Founding Fathers; human beings; legal fiction

Gans, David H., and Ilya Shapiro. *Religious Liberties for Corporations?: Hobby Lobby, the Affordable Care Act, and the Constitution*. New York: Palgrave Macmillan, 2014. DOI: 10.1057/9781137479709.0004.

DOI: 10.1057/9781137479709.0004

Jeffrey Rosen: We have a hard question to talk about today.[1] Indeed, the *Hobby Lobby* case has raised a couple of really difficult questions. First and most broadly: "Do corporations have the same religious freedom rights under the First Amendment as individuals do?" And, secondarily: "Does the mandate in the Affordable Care Act that requires for-profit corporations to provide contraceptive coverage—although it makes an exception for some religious institutions—violate both the First Amendment and also the Religious Freedom Restoration Act, which is a law Congress passed that provides many of the same protections as the First Amendment?" It sounds a bit technical but it's extremely important. It ties into the broader question that is transfixing the country over whether corporations have the same First Amendment rights in general as individuals do. The Supreme Court put that question front and center in *Citizens United v. FEC*, in which a five-justice majority said that corporations and natural persons do have the same free speech rights when it comes to campaign finance reform.[2] The question before the Court in the *Hobby Lobby* case is whether the rights of corporations and individuals are the same for the purposes of the free exercise of religion portion of the First Amendment, as well as the free speech part. So that's the broad question. We are just going to learn together because, like all hard constitutional questions, there are no easy answers to this one and our two panelists are going to illuminate us on this hard question.

Before we discuss the issues specific to the *Hobby Lobby* case, let's start with foundational principles about the Constitution and corporations. David, what, in your view, does the Constitution's text and history tell us about the rights of corporations?

David H. Gans: The Constitution does not give corporations the same protection of rights and liberties as it gives to individuals.[3] As its opening words reflect, the Constitution was written for the benefit of "We the People of the United States." It never specifically mentions corporations or accords them any explicit legal protections. Shortly after ratification, the Framers added the Bill of Rights to the Constitution to protect the fundamental rights of the citizens of the new nation, reflecting the promise of the Declaration of Independence that all Americans "are endowed by their Creator with certain unalienable rights, [and] that among these are life, liberty, and the pursuit of happiness."[4] Again, the Framers of the Bill of Rights made no explicit mention of corporations.

DOI: 10.1057/9781137479709.0004

The failure to mention corporations in the Constitution was purposeful. While the Constitution "declare[d] the great rights of mankind"[5] in the Bill of Rights, the one attempt to make a specific provision in the Constitution for corporations—a proposal to give Congress an enumerated power to charter corporations—was defeated. In voting down the proposed incorporation power, the Framers voiced worries that giving the federal government the power to create corporations, and conferring on them special privileges denied to the rest of the citizenry, would lead to excessive corporate power. Far from viewing corporations simply as a part of "We the People," the Framers worried about the vast powers that corporations might wield if a charter power were added to the Constitution.[6]

Indeed, at the Founding, corporations stood on an entirely different footing than living persons. A corporation, in the words of Chief Justice John Marshall, "is an artificial being, invisible, intangible, and existing only in the contemplation of the law. Being the creature of the law, it possesses only those properties which the charter of creation confers upon it, either expressly, or as incidental to its very existence. These are such as are supposed best calculated to effect the object for which it was created."[7] As early as the First Congress, James Madison summed up the founding-era vision of corporations: "[A] charter of incorporation...creates an artificial person not existing in law. It confers important civil rights and attributes, which could not otherwise be claimed."[8] In short, corporations, unlike the individual citizens that made up the nation, did not have fundamental and inalienable rights by virtue of their inherent dignity.

Far from considering corporations as persons deserving equal treatment with individuals, from the Founding on, corporations have been treated as uniquely powerful artificial entities—created and given special privileges to fuel economic growth—that necessarily must be subject to substantial government regulation in service of the public good. Fears that corporations would use their special privileges to overwhelm and undercut the rights of living Americans are as old as the Republic itself, and have been voiced throughout American history by some of our greatest statesmen, including James Madison, Thomas Jefferson, Andrew Jackson, Abraham Lincoln, Theodore Roosevelt, Franklin Delano Roosevelt, and others.[9]

Debates about the rights of business corporations—which are never mentioned in our Constitution, yet play an ever-expanding role in American

DOI: 10.1057/9781137479709.0004

society—have raged since the Framing era. The Supreme Court's answer to this question has long been a nuanced one: corporations can sue and be sued in federal court and they can assert certain constitutional rights, chiefly related to their right to enter into contracts, own and possess property, and manage their affairs, but they have never been accorded all the rights that individuals possess.[10]

Many of the constitutional rights possessed by business corporations are grounded in matters of property and commerce, reflecting the Supreme Court's view that "[c]orporations are a necessary feature of modern business activity" and that "[i]n organizing itself as a collective body, it waives no constitutional immunities appropriate to such body. Its property cannot be taken without compensation. It can only be proceeded against by due process of law, and is protected, under the 14th Amendment, against unlawful discrimination."[11] Business corporations enjoy other constitutional rights, but these rights do not vindicate a corporation's own claim to what is essentially human autonomy or dignity. For example, corporations enjoy rights under the Free Speech Clause, not because they enjoy personal dignity or freedom of conscience like people do, but because of the fundamental role that speech plays in our democracy. As the Court explained in *Citizens United*, business corporations have a constitutional right to speak because speech paid for by corporations helps to inform the general public and provide a robust debate for individual listeners.[12]

Because corporations do not possess the same dignity and conscience as individuals, some constitutional guarantees—even ones whose wording protects all "persons"—do not apply to business corporations. For example, the Fifth Amendment's Self-Incrimination Clause, which provides that no person shall be "compelled in any criminal case to be a witness against himself" does not protect business corporations because the Fifth Amendment right "is an explicit right of a natural person, protecting the realm of human thought and expression."[13] In the Fifth Amendment context, "there is a clear distinction . . . between an individual and a corporation. . . . While an individual may lawfully refuse to answer incriminating questions . . ., it does not follow that a corporation, vested with special privileges and franchises, may refuse to show its hand when charged with an abuse of such privileges."[14] Thus, since the Founding, corporations have been treated differently than individuals when it comes to certain fundamental, personal rights, and the Constitution's guarantees cannot be applied wholesale to corporations.

DOI: 10.1057/9781137479709.0004

Ilya Shapiro: Of course, it's true that a corporation is not a real person and that some constitutional rights—such as the protection for sexual privacy or prohibition on slavery—make no sense as applied to corporations. Even though a corporation isn't a living, breathing, blood-pumping human being, however, the individuals who make up those corporations—officers, directors, employees, shareholders—are. It would be a mistake to deny constitutional rights to those individuals on the grounds that the corporation itself isn't a real person. The rhetorical tactic of conflating a right with the means used to exercise it is just that—a tactic that misses the larger point: the people who own and operate the corporation are natural, rights-bearing individuals. Simply because a group of individuals decide to join together and exercise those rights in concert does not result in those individuals losing their rights. Stated another way, individuals standing together as a group shouldn't be stripped of rights that would be constitutionally guaranteed to them standing alone.[15]

The contention that the Constitution doesn't protect individuals organized as a corporation ignores the absence of a constitutional distinction between individuals and groups of individuals, however associated. People are free to organize and associate in a whole host of manners and the decision to use the corporate form—as opposed to a partnership, a union, a private club, or an informal group of friends—to pool their assets does not strip them of constitutional rights such as the freedom of speech.

Indeed, common sense tells us that corporations must have *some* constitutional rights—or there would be little incentive to form them in the first place. For example, if corporations had no right to be free from unreasonable search and seizure, the police could storm corporate offices and cart off computers and files for any or no reason. If corporations had no property rights, the mayor of New York could exercise eminent domain over Rockefeller Center by fiat and without compensation if he decides he'd like to move his office there. If forming a corporation means losing all of these (and other) constitutional protections, the only form of business would be sole proprietorships and the proverbial Mom 'n' Pop shops.

Similar to the above Fourth and Fifth Amendment examples, the Constitution has to protect the First Amendment rights of people associated through the corporate form. But that corporate form doesn't create new constitutional rights; it's simply a vehicle through which individuals exercise their own rights. "[T]he Court has long understood

DOI: 10.1057/9781137479709.0004

that to speak effectively in a vast nation, you need to be able to pool your resources with others."[16] The Court has recognized this within the realm of the right to expressive association, and corporate speech is but one form of expressive association. As Chief Justice Roberts said in his concurrence in *Citizens United*, "the First Amendment protects more than just the individual on a soapbox and the lone pamphleteer."[17]

Finally, the invocation of corporations during the Founding or early Republic is inapt because at that time, and actually dating back to ancient times, corporations were more like what we would now consider to be quasi-governmental public utilities than modern businesses. They got a charter from the government—the famous royal charters in England— that represented a monopoly in a given industry or geographic tract. The modern business corporation, on the other hand, doesn't so much get permission to operate from the government as exists at the nexus of contracts between various individual actors, one that is recognized by the law to facilitate commerce and other lawful activity by rights-bearing individuals. Unlike in James Madison's and John Marshall's day, we do recognize corporations as legal persons with certain rights. Even the great Chief Justice John Marshall, while noting that corporations are artificial beings in that *Dartmouth College* case that David quoted from, nevertheless in that case ruled for that (pre-modern) corporation in its dispute with the state.

The question, then, is: what is the scope of corporate rights? I suggest that they're a subset of those which natural persons have, and we protect them precisely to fully protect the rights and freedoms of those natural persons. So I fully agree with David's opening statement that the Constitution—and federal law more broadly, for that matter—doesn't give corporations the same rights as individuals. Where we disagree is which rights it does give them, what should happen when they clash with other rights or interests, and how to apply those understandings to specific cases such as *Citizens United* (political speech) or *Hobby Lobby* (religious exercise).

Notes

1   This and the next chapter are based on a National Constitution Center forum held on December 10, 2013.

DOI: 10.1057/9781137479709.0004

2   558 U.S. 310 (2010).

3   For a fuller discussion, see David H. Gans & Douglas T. Kendall, A Capitalist Joker: The Strange Origins, Disturbing Past, and Uncertain Future of Corporate Personhood in American Law (2010), available at http://theusconstitution.org/think-tank/narrative/capitalist-joker-corporations-corporate-personhood-and-constitution.

4   Decl. of Independence.

5   Annals of Congress, 1ˢᵗ Cong., 1ˢᵗ Sess. 449 (1789).

6   *See* Daniel Crane, Antitrust Antifederalism, 96 *Cal. L. Rev.* 1, 7–10 (2008).

7   *Trustees of Dartmouth College v. Woodward*, 17 U.S. (4 Wheat.) 518, 636 (1819).

8   Annals of Congress, 1st Cong., 3rd Sess. 1949 (1791).

9   *See generally* A Capitalist Joker, *supra.*

10   *Compare Dartmouth College, supra* (protection under Contracts Clause); *Louisville, Cincinnati & Charleston R. Co. v. Letson*, 43 U.S. (2 How.) 397 (1844) (right to sue under Article III); *Gloucester Ferry Co. v. Pennsylvania*, 114 U.S. 196 (1885) (protection under Dormant Commerce Clause); *Gulf, C. & S.F. Ry. Co. v. Ellis*, 165 U.S. 150 (1897) (protection under Equal Protection Clause); *Hale v. Henkel*, 201 U.S. 43 (1906) (protection under Fourth Amendment) *with Bank of Augusta v. Earle*, 38 U.S. (13 Pet.) 519 (1839) (no protection under Article IV's Privileges and Immunities Clause); *Hale, supra* (no protection under Fifth Amendment's Self-Incrimination Clause); *Western Turf Ass'n v. Greenberg*, 204 U.S. 359 (1907) (no protection under Fourteenth Amendment's Privileges or Immunities Clause); *United States v. Morton Salt Co.*, 338 U.S. 632, 652 (1950) (observing that "corporations can claim no equality with individuals in the enjoyment of a right to privacy").

11   *Hale*, 201 U.S. at 76.

12   *Citizens United*, 558 U.S. at 349.

13   *Braswell v. United States*, 487 U.S. 99, 119 (1988) (Kennedy, J., dissenting). The majority opinion in *Braswell* made a similar point, explaining that "for purposes of the Fifth Amendment, corporations and other collective entities are treated differently than individuals." *Id.* at 104.

14   *Hale*, 201 U.S. at 74, 75.

15   For fuller discussion of these points, see Ilya Shapiro & Caitlin W. McCarthy, So What If Corporations Aren't People, 44 *John Marshall L. Rev.* 701 (2011).

16   Eugene Volokh, Constitutional Rights and Corporations, *The Volokh Conspiracy* (September 22, 2009), http://volokh.com/posts/1253637850.shtml.

17   *Citizens United*, 558 U.S. at 373 (Roberts, C.J., concurring).

2
Corporate Personhood and Religious Liberty

Abstract: *This chapter examines the claim at the heart of* Hobby Lobby: *do corporations have a right to exercise religion? Gans says no, because this is a personal right tied to conscience, conviction, and human dignity. No court has ever protected the right of businesses to practice religion. On the contrary, courts have refused to grant secular corporations religious exemptions, particularly from laws protecting employees' rights. Shapiro disagrees because the people behind the company can have their religious liberty violated through actions affecting the corporation. Neither legal form nor profit motive affects the scope of individual rights; the proper inquiry under the law is whether religious exercise is burdened, whether the government can justify that burden, and whether there's another way to achieve its justified goal.*

Keywords: First Amendment; freedom of conscience; free exercise; religious exemptions; religious liberty; RFRA

Gans, David H., and Ilya Shapiro. *Religious Liberties for Corporations?: Hobby Lobby, the Affordable Care Act, and the Constitution.* New York: Palgrave Macmillan, 2014. DOI: 10.1057/9781137479709.0005.

Jeffrey Rosen: You've now agreed that corporations have some rights but disagreed over the scope of those rights and how to apply them. So let's now turn to the right to freely exercise religion, which is at the core of *Hobby Lobby*. David, you filed a brief in this case arguing that the framers of the First Amendment would not have intended corporations to have the same religious liberty rights as natural persons. Tell us more about that argument.

David H. Gans: The text, history, and purpose of the constitutional guarantee of the free exercise of religion all make clear that secular, for-profit corporations cannot claim to exercise religion. The Framers rooted the free exercise right in fundamentally human attributes—reason, conviction, and conscience—that make little sense as applied to corporations.

The fundamental right that the free exercise guarantee protects is a personal one. The debates over the Free Exercise Clause, the plethora of state constitutions that were drafted that influenced the Framing era's understanding of the free exercise right, and James Madison's iconic statements about religious liberty all demonstrate that the free exercise right is a fundamental protection of conscience, conviction, and human dignity.[1] Those attributes don't apply to and cannot be invoked by business corporations. In short, the Framers understood the free exercise right to be an inalienable human right of the kind that was described in the Declaration of Independence, a fundamental protection of conscience and dignity that does not extend to business corporations.

Two other points are critical. First, in over two centuries, the Supreme Court has never said that the free exercise right protects business corporations and, until these disputes, there has not even been a suggestion that secular, for-profit corporations can exercise religion. This reflects that there is a fundamental difference between "We the People" and business corporations when it comes to these matters of conscience and human dignity. Further, when the Supreme Court has interpreted other fundamental, personal rights of human dignity and conscience, it has consistently held that those protections do not extend to corporations. Thus, while business corporations have a number of rights under the Constitution, there are some—particularly ones that protect human dignity—that they don't possess.

And second, Hobby Lobby's free exercise claim is particularly troubling because it would give a corporation's owners the power to impose their

DOI: 10.1057/9781137479709.0005

own religious views on their employees who have deeply held convictions of their own and may want and need access to a full range of FDA-approved contraceptives, including the IUD, which is both the most expensive and most effective form of contraception. For this reason, the case raises the question of whose religious liberty is at issue and how should courts deal with the competing claims of corporate CEOs and the employees? In past cases on religious liberty, the Supreme Court has repeatedly found that a religious exemption should not be granted when it would allow a business owner to impose his or her religious views on employees. That's precisely the case here. Granting an exemption to Hobby Lobby would deny female employees important federal rights to contraceptive coverage protected by the Affordable Care Act.

Rosen: Wonderful. So Ilya, David made three broad points. One was about the original understanding of the Framers, the second about Supreme Court precedent, and the third about the practical consequence of recognizing this right. Let's hone in on the original understanding argument first. David basically says that the Framers thought of religious freedom that comes from God and not government. James Madison believed that we couldn't alienate this natural right because our religious beliefs are the product of external impressions operating on our minds; religious worship was a duty and that's why there was a corresponding right that couldn't be alienated. David says that can't belong to corporations. It has to belong to natural persons. What's the response to that?

Ilya Shapiro: Well, that's true to a point. Whatever rights corporations have, whether in the religious area, in political speech, or anything else, aren't due to their being legal persons. As Chief Justice Marshall explained in that *Dartmouth College* case that David previously quoted, corporations are formed by individuals and those individuals have constitutional rights, including the right to pursue some greater good.[2] In other words, corporate rights derive from the rights of the natural persons of which they are composed.[3] We don't create new rights or beings that have new rights when we create or recognize corporations or any other types of associations: limited liability companies (LLCs), partnerships, unions, private clubs, non-profits like Cato and CAC, or even a unique institution like the National Constitution Center. All of these different organizations are conglomerations of people who have rights to a certain extent, so I don't think David goes so far—at least I hope he doesn't—as to say that when people get together in the corporate form,

DOI: 10.1057/9781137479709.0005

they lose their rights. Or even that the corporations they form have no rights whatsoever. For example, the police couldn't raid IBM and take all their computers and files without a warrant because the corporation has Fourth Amendment rights.[4] The mayor of New York couldn't move his office to Rockefeller Center and therefore take over NBC's studios without paying just compensation because the corporate owners of the property have Fifth Amendment rights.[5] So really what this discussion is about is the extent of particular kinds of rights—in this case the religious liberties of individuals—and how they work in the corporate form.

Again, it's kind of tricky dealing with all this from an originalist perspective because corporations as we know them—modern corporations or other types of business associations—didn't exist in the Founding Era. Whenever you come across the idea of a corporation from Thomas Jefferson or others of the time, they're talking about government-granted monopolies like the British East India Company or Hudson's Bay Company, or other sorts of government-granted corporate charters—kind of a quasi-governmental agency I guess you could call them. Maybe the closest thing that we have now would be a Fannie Mae or a Freddie Mac, or the postal service, maybe Amtrak. It's not your typical modern for-profit corporation. So the real inquiry here is whether individual rights, in this case religious liberties, are being unduly violated under the Religious Freedom Restoration Act (RFRA) or under the First Amendment—those are, of course, separate questions—when the government makes certain demands of corporations that are closely tied to those individuals.

Rosen: Great. David, this is a powerful response Ilya makes. He says that the Framers couldn't have thought about corporations in the modern sense because those didn't exist and we need to translate the Framers' notion of individual liberty to a world where individuals aggregate together. Is it your position that corporations have no rights or do you just believe that if I run a for-profit corporation and I'm religiously motivated, I should sue in my personal capacity as the D.C. Circuit held?[6] That court didn't say that you can't come into court. They just said that the owners of the corporation in that case, Freshway Foods, and their fellow plaintiffs should sue and assert their rights as individuals. Is that the only difference between your positions?

Gans: I hope I didn't hear Ilya making a living-constitutionalist argument here. Everyone recognizes that corporations have changed immensely since the Founding era. But our fundamental constitutional principles

DOI: 10.1057/9781137479709.0005

have not. My argument here focuses on the nature of the free exercise right and whether its protections—rooted in conscience and human dignity—extend to secular, for-profit businesses like Hobby Lobby. There are certain rights in the Constitution that have extended to corporations. Ilya mentioned the Fourth Amendment as an example, and I think that one's not controversial. But, even in that context, the Court has recognized that corporations are not entitled to the same rights as individuals. The issue that *Hobby Lobby* raises, however, is the scope and meaning of the constitutional guarantee of free exercise of religion—and it's profound because for over two centuries the Supreme Court has never said that business corporations have had religious free exercise rights, which are closely tied to human dignity and conscience. In fact, the Supreme Court has never said—not even in *Citizens United*—that rights of human dignity belong equally to individuals and business corporations. So the key question, I think, is the nature of the right. If you look at that Founding understanding—which, again, is still very much our understanding in the sense that religious free exercise is a protection of conscience and human dignity—those rights do not extend to business corporations for the reason that corporations don't pray. They don't express pious devotion to a god. They don't have a religious conscience.

Of course, corporations are different now, but that's ultimately besides the point. You can look at the whole sweep of American history and the evolution of the business corporation model, and throughout that whole history there has never been a claim that business corporations are "persons" exercising religion. That's really the core question before the Supreme Court. It would really be a momentous break from both the foundational text and history as well as the whole sweep of American history to say that business corporations have the same rights as "We the People" to engage in acts of free religious exercise. Corporations have some rights but the Supreme Court has recognized that corporations do not have all the rights individuals possess. When you're dealing with purely personal rights that inhere in human dignity and conscience, those rights are guaranteed to individuals and not to business corporations.

Rosen: So the strong response is, first, the precedent point again. David says that the Supreme Court has never before recognized a secular, for-profit corporation as having rights under the Free Exercise Clause. That's also the claim of the Obama administration. Is that correct as a matter of precedent? My understanding is that Jewish merchants in the 20th century did challenge Sunday closing laws—but I think they lost, as it happens. Tell us more about that history.

Shapiro: That case, *Braunfeld v. Brown*,[8] was curious. Jewish merchants in Pennsylvania—I'm not sure what their exact corporate form was, but it's actually not important—challenged Sunday closing laws. Of course, for Jews, Saturday is the Sabbath. These plaintiffs said that, because of their religion, they have to close on Saturday, but now the government was forcing them to close also on Sunday. So they could only operate five days a week, which naturally put them at a competitive disadvantage in relation to competitors who could operate six days a week. They did ultimately lose their free exercise, establishment clause, and equal protection claims, but the Court was badly divided with Chief Justice Warren writing for a plurality of four justices, and Justice Felix Frankfurter and John Marshall Harlan concurring separately and sort of hemming and hawing on the fence. In rejecting the free exercise claim, Chief Justice Earl Warren wrote that the plaintiffs' religious rights were indeed violated (indirectly) but that there was no other way for the government to achieve its goal of a universal day of rest.[10]

Notably, just two years later, Justice William Brennan, who was in dissent in *Braunfeld*, wrote the majority opinion in the seminal case of *Sherbert v. Verner*, in which the Court struck down on free exercise grounds a law that prohibited a worker from collecting unemployment compensation who was terminated from her job because she couldn't work on Saturdays for religious reasons. So *Braunfeld* didn't turn on what *kind* of business was asserting rights, or even if it was the business exercising religion or those who ran it. It's not a precedent one way or another regarding corporate rights, but instead is the opening bookend to the Court's *Sherbert v. Verner* religious-accommodation period. The other bookend of course came in 1990 with Justice Antonin Scalia's majority opinion in *Employment Division v. Smith*, which held that the Free Exercise Clause generally doesn't require the government to provide religious accommodations or exemptions to religiously motivated individuals.[12]

Other cases that followed *Sherbert*—which many in Congress cited favorably when passing RFRA in response to *Smith*—seem to suggest that if the government forced a business owner to open on the Sabbath or actively do certain things against his or her religious beliefs, that would amount to a constitutional violation.[13] Again, it's not the corporate form that matters, but the rights of people who act through the corporate

DOI: 10.1057/9781137479709.0005

form—in terms of social responsibility or whatever type of guiding mission they want their business to have. And, indeed, in modern law, every jurisdiction in America says that corporations can pursue *any lawful purpose*.[14] It's safe to say that people don't lose their rights when they begin to operate in a commercial manner or when they incorporate.

The point I'm making here is that nobody is disputing that corporations *qua* corporations don't pray or believe in God or get down on their knees, or any of these sorts of things. They don't even have knees, right? It's not a point about anthropomorphizing corporations, but, clearly, in practical terms, if you mandate a corporation to do something that its owners find religiously offensive, it doesn't matter if it's a corporation acting versus its owners in their individual capacities. In a very real sense, the question of whether a corporation can assert a religious-liberty claim is academic because, regardless how you articulate the legalese, it's human individuals who feel a burden on their religious exercise.[15]

Let me quote for you footnote 14 from the Third Circuit case, *Conestoga Wood*—the companion case to *Hobby Lobby* that's also before the Court:

> The majority thinks it important that corporations lack the anthropomorphic qualities of individual devotion. "They do not pray, serve sacraments or take other religiously motivated actions separate and apart from the intentions and directions of their individual actors." Of course corporations do not picket, or march on Capitol Hill, or canvas door to door for moral causes either, but the majority would not claim that corporations do not have First Amendment rights to free speech or to petition the government. Corporations have those rights not because they have arms and legs but because the people who form and operate them do. We are concerned in this case with people even when they operate in the particular form of association called a corporation. It is perhaps no accident that the only support that my colleagues put forward to show that a corporation's lack of body parts deprives it of religious liberty is a district court case that's been reversed, a dissent in a court of appeals case, and a dissent in a Supreme Court case. An argument that has lost three times is not necessarily wrong for that record but maybe the record says something about that argument.[16]

I think that, again, it's not a matter of when you're engaging in commercial activity, that's the dividing point—though that's certainly the position that the Obama administration takes. I don't think David has taken that position in the past because there are a host of other types of religious businesses—say, Christian bookstores—that are involved in commercial

DOI: 10.1057/9781137479709.0005

activity. Even the Catholic Church is involved in commercial activity to an extent. I guess there must be something peculiar to this corporate form that does it and I want to hear what exactly that is.

Rosen: Great, so help us understand this corporate form, David, because I don't quite get it yet and I think it's the key to the case. Ilya cites to Judge Kent Jordan's dissent in the Third Circuit's *Conestoga Wood* decision. The Third Circuit includes Pennsylvania and Judge Jordan is a neighbor, a judge right nearby, and he cited *Citizens United* for the proposition that corporations do have some constitutional liberties.[17] Is this corporate form question the only disagreement between the two of you? Even if the corporation can't sue in its collective capacity, would a bunch of individuals who own a corporation may be able to sue in their individual capacity and assert that their personal free exercise rights are being violated? If that's that case, is there much difference between your positions, or am I missing a wrinkle that makes the question of corporate form more complicated?

Gans: Let me start by going back to the Jewish merchant cases that Ilya started with. There have been, over the course of American history, a number of cases in which individual business owners have brought free exercise claims to the courts. A couple of them have made it all the way to the Supreme Court. These claims have been a complete failure. In case after case, the courts have rejected the efforts of commercial business owners to obtain religious exemptions from generally applicable business regulation.

The first of these is the 1961 ruling *Braunfeld v. Brown,* which we have discussed. In that case, the Supreme Court refused to "hold unassailable all legislation which imposes solely an indirect burden on religion," concluding that the constitutional guarantee of free exercise did not forbid establishing a "general day of rest" or require that a Jewish merchant be given a religious exemption.[18] There is a very important 1982 case called *United States v. Lee,* in which an Amish business owner sued to obtain an exemption from paying Social Security taxes for his employees, claiming that payments required to fund the Social Security system conflicted with Amish beliefs about self-sufficiency and community mutual aid.[19] In these cases, as in *Hobby Lobby,* the owners said that they just want to run their businesses according to the dictates of their faith. In all of these cases the Court rejected that claim. *Lee* is particularly important because the Court said that once you enter the business world, you can't think about religion in the same way. An exemption from Social Security would impose your religious belief on your employees, who don't have to be Amish and may very well need the benefits that Social Security provides.[20] In sum, Hobby Lobby's argument is truly unprecedented: the Supreme Court has never given business corporations religious free exercise rights and never accorded them the right to seek religious exemptions from general business regulation.

True, there's a distinction between the rights of business owners and the rights of business corporations, at least in some contexts. In that regard, one quite important body of case law is the Court's cases interpreting the Fifth Amendment's Self-Incrimination Clause, which for over a century the Supreme Court has said does not apply to businesses—and the reasoning of those cases has direct application to the *Hobby Lobby* case we're now discussing. As the Court has time and again explained, the Fifth Amendment's constitutional privilege against self-incrimination, much like the free exercise right, concerns conscience and human dignity, and those protections do not apply to business corporations.[21] An individual business owner who is not incorporated can assert an objection based on the privilege against self-incrimination, but a business corporation can't. A business owner can't say, "Well, in my individual capacity, I have a privilege against self-incrimination." The Supreme Court has rejected that claim. When you're acting on behalf of the corporation, you are not acting in an individual capacity, you are acting for the company. As the Court explained, the individual owner cannot "be said to be exercising [his] personal rights and duties nor to be entitled to [his] purely personal privileges."[22] Instead, he "assume[d] the rights, duties and privileges of the artificial entity."[23] In short, whatever rights an individual owner might have are corporate rights. That's why the key question is the nature of the right, and the free exercise right is very much about human dignity and individual conscience. It's not a right that secular, for-profit corporations possess.

Moreover, there is a fundamental distinction between the free exercise right and the free speech right at issue in *Citizens United*. First, the issue in *Citizens United* was not whether corporations have rights under the free speech clause. The Supreme Court said that they do many years before *Citizens United*.[24] The issue instead was whether corporations have the *same* rights as individuals. And, on that question, the Court said yes by a vote of 5–4, and the main reason was that any speech—especially about a candidate's fitness for office (there it was about Hillary Clinton, whom Citizens United thought wouldn't be a good president)—benefits human listeners and enriches democracy. The reasoning relied very heavily on the rights of the audience, concluding that any limitation on independent political speech deprives listeners of speech on important political matters.

In *Hobby Lobby*, on the other hand, the focus is very much on the relationship between the individual and God and matters of conscience—and that forces you to ask whether a business corporation can be treated as a person exercising religion. For the reasons I already argued, I do not think that the fundamental protections of the free exercise of religion—which protect human dignity and freedom of conscience—extends to secular, for-profit corporations such as Hobby Lobby. This is one of those contexts in which business corporations do not have the same rights that individuals possess.

The fundamental point is that corporations cannot have their cake and eat it too, claiming all the special privileges given to corporations and all the fundamental, personal rights granted to individuals, including rights given to protect freedom of conscience and human dignity for individuals. A business owner cannot go back and forth between individual and corporate status to gain the benefits of both; with the sweet of special privileges comes greater government regulation to ensure that corporations do not abuse their privileges. Or, as the Third Circuit in *Conestoga Wood* explained, corporate owners "cannot move freely between corporate and individual status to gain the advantages and avoid the disadvantages of the respective forms."[25]

This fundamental principle about corporate rights goes back to some of the earliest foundational precedents on the rights of corporations. In the 1839 case of *Bank of Augusta v. Earle*,[26] the Court said corporations were not entitled to the privileges and immunities of citizens protected by Article IV of the Constitution. The Court reasoned that if a corporation wanted to be considered as an individual carrying on a business and thus entitled to the privileges and immunities of citizenship, then it should also have to take on the liabilities of an individual.[27] That same reasoning applies in the *Hobby Lobby* case. Hobby Lobby should not be entitled to be treated as a corporation for purposes of receiving special corporate privileges—protections such as limited liability that no individuals may obtain—but as an individual when it comes to fundamental personal

DOI: 10.1057/9781137479709.0005

rights, such as the free exercise right, designed to secure human dignity and protect freedom of conscience for all Americans. That would be a fundamental perversion of fundamental constitutional as well as corporate law principles.

Rosen: Great, that's quite an extensive answer. So Ilya, he's not saying that they have no rights, just that they don't have the same rights. He's given a couple of examples where the Supreme Court has said if the right involves human dignity like the Fifth Amendment, where the Framers are centrally concerned with not putting an individual under oath and forcing him to choose between self-incrimination and eternal damnation or contempt of court. That's why you don't force an individual to go under oath, but you can't have a corporation blaspheme itself to eternal damnation, so corporations don't have the same Fifth Amendment rights as individuals. What's your response to the claim that corporations have some Bill of Rights protections, but not all the same ones.

Shapiro: Sure, I agree that corporations don't have souls.

Rosen: You've never met Google.

Shapiro: Right, Google says "don't be evil," which is their corporate mantra. They try to conduct their business in a way that doesn't promote evil. That might be a far-fetched example, especially given that Google is now a public company and there are questions with regard to our analysis about how much its founders control and whether all the interests are aligned. But in Hobby Lobby's case, it's quite clear that objecting to the contraceptive mandate isn't some kind of isolated circumstance. There are a host of policies they've put in place to abide by their religious faith. For example, they don't allow back-shipments of beer on their delivery trucks. They don't sell shot glasses in their stores. They play what they consider to be positive, life-affirming music. There's a whole way in which they conduct their business according to their faith.

Indeed, lots of business owners have some sort of guiding principle beyond just making money. Take Starbucks, which has its own mantra about fair-trade coffee. What if the coffee producers lobbied Congress and obtained a law requiring all coffee shops to sell a certain type of coffee that's not necessarily fair trade. At that point, Starbucks can't conduct its business the way it wants. Is that a religious issue implicating RFRA and the Free Exercise Clause? I don't know, but if you take these sorts of mandates to their ultimate conclusion, you have a lot of interference

DOI: 10.1057/9781137479709.0005

with the belief systems of those who run corporations. And again, it's not so much about the corporation. The corporation is an inanimate legal fiction. It's the people who own and run the company.

In this case, if Hobby Lobby or Conestoga doesn't comply with this mandate, they're going to be fined an astronomical amount. For Hobby Lobby, based on their large number of employees, that'll be $1.3 million per day ($100 per day per affected individual). That fine, ultimately, comes out of the pockets of the individual owners who control these companies.

I'm not trying to draw a distinction between closely held companies and public companies—the religious claim might be harder to make for companies with millions of shareholders, and it would surely be much rarer than with a closely held family company—because regardless we have to observe the legal structures and the individual freedom they enable. For example, one reason that we have corporations is so if the company hurts someone—or is hurt itself—you don't have to have millions of shareholders as co-plaintiffs or co-defendants. Such a legal mechanism also facilitates commerce, or facilitates transactions. But then when it comes to the assertion of corporate rights, what you need to look at is whether any given asserted right ultimately protects individuals, whence all rights originate. Just like having the Fifth Amendment protection against self-incrimination for the corporation doesn't do anything for the individuals, maintaining this protection in the context of religious exercise *does* help the individuals promote and preserve their own liberties.

I agree with the cases that David mentioned. And I agreed with Chief Justice John Roberts when he wrote for a unanimous Court a couple of terms ago in the *FCC v. AT&T* case, denying the idea that corporations have privacy rights in a particular statutory context. His last line was clever: "I hope AT&T doesn't take this personally."[28] And again, that's true.

I agree with David that corporations don't have the same rights as individuals, so what we're debating is the scope of these rights. I don't have much of a dog in the fight about whether the ultimate jurisprudence should see religious liberties as a "pass-through right" going from the corporation to the individual or whether it should be framed as the individual suing in his own capacity, even though the mandate applies to the corporation directly. However lawyers and judges want to articulate that is fine with me but the ultimate point is that we have these constitutional protections to protect individual liberty and you don't lose those when you form corporations.

Finally, I think what I'm hearing from David is that you don't necessarily lose your rights when you engage in commercial activity because individuals can engage in commercial activity. But I don't know what there is that's special about a particular type of business structure, and why your rights change when you move from a sole proprietorship, to a partnership, to an LLC, to a corporation. I readily admit that corporations don't have all the rights of individuals, precisely because they're not individuals and it would be silly to think of a corporation's right to abortion or other similar examples. But concretely here, to protect that individual exercise of liberty you have to protect it in the corporate form.

Rosen: Just wanted to follow up if I may, so I can understand the difference between the individual and the corporation suing. Say Larry Page at Google hears a calling and decides to embrace Jesus Christ as his savior and run Google along Christian principles and promote Bibles in the cafeteria and so forth. Could he then sue in his individual capacity for an exemption, not only from the contraception mandate, but from all federal regulations that he believes violates his religious beliefs, including refusing to cover stem cell research or participating in Obamacare altogether?

Shapiro: Or only hiring people of his faith.

Rosen: Exactly. Basically he wants exemption from federal laws prohibiting discrimination on the basis of religion and gender for all of Google because he's says they violate his religious liberty. Would he be entitled to the exemption?

Shapiro: Well, I don't think Larry Page still has majority control of the company. There would have to be a complicated test about whether what he's pushing really is part of the company's mission, whether it's just that one shareholder—not even a majority asserting that their rights are violated. You could have one share and disagree, from a religious perspective among many others, with what the company is doing. And the solution there may well be, sorry, just sell that share. It may well be possible to have a publicly traded for-profit corporation with a religious mission. It would have to comply with all the securities laws by disclosing to potential investors during its IPO (initial public offering) that the business would be run in a certain way, but theoretically it could be done. Which doesn't mean that the religious objection would always trump; we can't have Azteca, Inc., performing human sacrifices, for example. But under the existing rubric of RFRA's overlay on the First Amendment, courts would have to weigh the usual considerations about the extent of the law's burden on religion, the strength of the government interest, and whether the government uses the least-restrictive means of advancing that interest.

There was one recent corporation that won *unanimously* at the Supreme Court when the government tried to change its employment policies. This is the *Hosanna-Tabor* case where the Court ruled that, yes, a religiously denominated school could fire someone without regard to a certain federal employment law.[29] One of the school's tenets was that if you had a dispute with the management, you had to bring it to the intra-church arbitration process rather than suing. The plaintiff didn't do that when she had an issue regarding medical leave, so they fired her. The Court didn't get into questions of, for example, whether she was really more of a math teacher than a religion teacher. The justices said that they don't want courts getting involved in that sort of thing—weighing whether someone's job was "religious enough"—and, after all, even the Pope spends a great deal of his time on management and administration. Instead, there's a "ministerial exception" under which courts will take you at your word that some policy is part of your faith (assuming you sincerely believe it, rather than conjuring it up as a pretext during litigation; courts will certainly look into that). The Obama administration wanted to do away with the ministerial exemption altogether, but it couldn't get a single vote for that position—which makes sense, because I don't think we want to apply antidiscrimination laws such that Catholic churches have to consider Muslims for the position of priest, etc.

So it's a complicated inquiry—and a much more complicated inquiry for a large company, whether corporate or not—that looks at whether the organization has a sincere religious mission. Courts do not and should not get into theological decision making about the rationality or centrality of certain tenets to any given religious faith. Hard questions make for hard law. Perhaps we may come to the big Google question at some point, but certainly for closely held companies like Hobby Lobby—which can get quite big, so this isn't simply about size—there's no question that all of their shareholders are feeling religious injury.

DOI: 10.1057/9781137479709.0005

Rosen: David, what's your response to this idea? It might be a complicated test but it could be appropriate to examine if and when a Larry Page finds religion and controls enough of Google to get these exemptions. And what about this *Hosanna-Tabor* case that Ilya mentioned, which granted a ministerial exemption?

Gans: Ilya said a lot of different things. Let me try to respond, and hit some of the highlights. I'm glad he invoked *Hosanna-Tabor* because that case raises a lot of very important points, which are quite important in *Hobby Lobby* and which we have not touched on as of yet.

First, having a mantra does not make you a person who exercises religion or allow you to invoke the free exercise right. It just shows you how hard it is to make the case that corporations have rights of conscience and human dignity to exercise religion in the same way that living, breathing humans do. Second, it's very important to focus on *how* Hobby Lobby and their fellow plaintiffs claim to exercise religion in this case. The owners of these corporations want to impose their religious views on their employees, who may not share that view. After all, when you work at Hobby Lobby, you don't have to subscribe to the same view as the owners. (I suppose if you did, that would be a separate case—which may well come up in future if the corporation is successful here.) Hobby Lobby hires across religious faiths, but when it comes to the Affordable Care Act's requirement of contraceptive coverage, the company insists that its employees are not allowed to have this important federal right that the law provides to ensure that female employees and their families have access to a full range of contraceptives.

Some of the examples that Jeff raised demonstrate that there's no real stopping point to Hobby Lobby's claim that secular business should be entitled to a religious exemption from generally applicable laws designed to protect the rights of their employees. Can a business corporation, when faced with a same-sex married couple who wants to exercise their rights under the Family and Medical Leave Act to take care of an adopted child, say that it has a religious objection to same-sex marriage and therefore it won't provide that leave, demanding a religious exemption from that law? Could a Muslim employer decide not to pay for insurance coverage for any medication that involves the use of pig derivatives, or perhaps a heart transplant involving a pig? And finally, as Jeff's hypothetical about Google asked, can a corporation claim a religious exemption from federal civil rights laws that protect Americans from discrimination? That's

DOI: 10.1057/9781137479709.0005

an issue that has been hotly debated in the states recently in the context of LGBT discrimination.[30]

Once you decide that a for-profit secular employer can say that providing rights to their employees violates their own corporate conscience and requires an exemption, you're transforming the way business corporations work and affecting the rights of employees across a huge number of contexts. You make it easier for employers to discriminate against employees who don't adhere to their religious code, which turns the idea of religious liberty on its head.

And finally, let me get to *Hosanna-Tabor* because it connects to this point. *Hosanna-Tabor* deals with a religious employer, a school affiliated with the Lutheran Church. *Hosanna-Tabor* concludes that a church can hire its own, at least when it comes to ministers. Chief Justice John Roberts, in his opinion for the Court, concludes that the text and history of the First Amendment "shows a special solicitude to the rights of religious organizations."[31] The question in *Hobby Lobby* is whether the Court will say that business corporations have the same rights as religious organizations, and extend the same solicitude to secular, for-profit corporations. If the justices properly reflect on our constitutional and corporate law traditions—which, again, go back to the Framing and the earliest corporate law[32]—they will recognize the fundamental difference between a business corporations formed to facilitate making a profit and religious ones, organized to encourage the flourishing of communal religious exercise.[33]

Hosanna-Tabor is one example of many where religious institutions receive legal protections for religious exercise, which have never been extended to secular businesses. In Title VII of the Civil Rights Act, for example, which is the main federal employment discrimination law, if you're a church, you can hire on the basis of religion, preferring persons who belong to the church.[34] And that's how a religious association stays a religious association; it hires its own believers in order to fulfill its mission—and Title VII permits it to do so, providing an exemption for religious corporations from Title VII's prohibition on religious discrimination.

No one has ever dreamed that the same freedom exists for business corporations. If Hobby Lobby or Google had a policy of hiring only Christian employees, that would be a patent violation of the Civil Rights Act. The

DOI: 10.1057/9781137479709.0005

claim made by Hobby Lobby is that secular businesses, too, deserve an exemption from laws that violate the religious beliefs of a company's owners. This is a far-reaching claim, which tears down the fundamental distinction between the religious rights of religious organizations, which have consistently been recognized, and the religious rights of business corporations, which never have. The Affordable Care Act's implementing regulations get our first principles exactly right because they recognize the case of religious employers as a special one—that religious organizations sometimes are entitled to religious exemptions, which have never been extended to business corporations.

Rosen: Just to understand that final point, the regulations implementing the Affordable Care Act provide an exemption to the contraception mandate for religious employers, narrowly defined to include houses of worship and their affiliates. There is also an accommodation provided to religiously affiliated non-profit organizations, and there is other litigation pending whether the accommodation itself violates RFRA. But the question in this case, in *Hobby Lobby*, is whether the definition of "religious organizations" is broad enough. And the challengers are saying "We shouldn't limit it to religious corporations, it should also include secular, for-profit corporations."

Ilya, as in any good, sophisticated NCC debate, David just made three points. First, he said the *Hosanna-Tabor* case is different; that was an exemption limited to a religious organization and it would be a stretch to extend it to a secular, for-profit business. Second, he said Hobby Lobby is attempting to impose the religious beliefs of the owners on the employees. Third, and most broadly, he said that this would really be a wedge into creating exemptions from a whole host of federal regulations. Judge Ilana Rovner, in her dissenting opinion in the Seventh Circuit case of *Korte v. Sebelius*, made this case too. Let me read an excerpt: "The Court's holding…has the potential to reach far beyond contraception and invite employers to take exemptions from any number of federally mandated employee benefits to which an employer might object on religious grounds."[35]

For example, Judge Rovner argued, a Methodist who objects—who objects to stem cell research might refuse to cover an employee's participation in a clinical trial of stem cell research for Lou Gehrig's Disease. A Christian Scientist employer could say that the mandate of coverage for traditional medical care violates his religious beliefs. And a southern Baptist employer who objects to gay marriage and surrogacy might refuse family leave to gay employees that would otherwise be required under federal law.[36]

Lots to chew on. What are your responses?

Shapiro: Well, in a pluralistic society, we can't have exemptions for everything. The test isn't simply—and shouldn't be—whether the law infringes on religious beliefs or practices and if it does then it can't be enforced. That's not the test and raising a religious objection to a generally applicable law is never the end of the legal analysis. Take the Social Security case, *Lee*; there are a lot of people who say that it violates their religious beliefs to pay taxes, or to pay that percentage of taxes that go towards making bombs, say (think of the pacifist Quakers). The government wins all those cases, and rightly so. You know, we get into some difficult issues here, but ultimately the test that the court applies now under RFRA is as follows: (1) Does a generally applicable law place a substantial burden on the exercise of religion? If it does, then (2) does the government nevertheless have a compelling interest it's trying to achieve in enforcing this law, burdensome as it may be? And finally, (3) is it pursuing this worthy goal in the most narrowly tailored way possible, such that there's no other means of getting there but through this law that unfortunately burdens religious practice? So there are lots of hoops to jump through before you get to win your exemption claim.

Some of the examples that have been raised might be real and might be hard cases, regarding not wanting to cover certain medical products or procedures. That's very similar to what's being claimed in *Hobby Lobby*. Other hypothetical cases probably fall on the outer edge of reality and of what courts will accept, like the family medical leave example—in that employees have family emergencies regardless of whether the relationship at the heart of that family is a marriage or not. There can be too much accommodation of religious minorities perhaps, such that the government can never enforce a generally applicable law. Or even too much accommodation of majorities, in a manner that violates the Establishment Clause. This intersection of law and religion is tricky.[38]

But getting back to the issue we're actually faced with, let me address a point that David's been arguing throughout, from his very opening statement: that Hobby Lobby and its owners are trying to impose their religious beliefs on their employees. It doesn't seem like that's what they're doing. They're not saying that they won't hire someone who uses contraceptives—generally or the ones at issue—or who won't pray with them, or won't donate to their church. They're not saying that they "disapprove" of certain behavior that employees engage in on their own time. There aren't anti-contraceptive inserts in the paycheck envelopes, or even posters on the wall in the lunch room saying, "don't use IUDs." Just as they were before Obamacare, the employees are free to go out and obtain whatever legal product they want. There's no issue of access to contraceptives. The only issue is whether the employer has to pay for them.

That issue only arose with the advent of Obamacare and its employer mandate. The Affordable Care Act is what created this controversy, this litigation. The Greens didn't all of a sudden decide that they were going to wage a "war on women"—that would be news to Barbara Green and all the other female co-owners of the businesses bringing these lawsuits—but instead it's the government that has decided to insinuate itself into women's health care decisions and force employers into the bedroom, as it were. Curiously, it's not at all clear that the ACA made access to contraceptives a full-fledged statutory right, given that employees can't sue their employer over it. Instead, it's the government that would be fining the employer or otherwise enforcing the regulatory scheme.

And a final point, on the religious versus non-religious business distinction. One of Hobby Lobby's co-plaintiffs is a company called Mardel, which is a Christian bookstore. It's not a church and it's not attached to a church; it's a for-profit business that sells Christian books. You could imagine also a kosher deli; there are plenty of purely commercial organizations that aren't engaged in social services. They're definitely for-profit—they're in it to make a buck—but they're also definitely identified with a religion and abide very explicitly by its tenets. You don't have to think hard to imagine a federal or state regulation that might conflict with those. So I don't think the dividing line is really for-profit versus non-profit. And nobody is saying that Mardel should be treated any differently than Hobby Lobby—that the secular/religious nature of the products you sell for a profit matter here. I guess that brings us back to corporate versus non-corporate (partnership, LLC, etc.) and for the reasons I've already outlined, I'm not sure how the *structure* of a business affects the rights of the individuals associated with that business. I'll leave it there.

DOI: 10.1057/9781137479709.0005

Rosen: Great, Ilya, and your response reminds me that we have talked a lot about the rights of corporations under the Constitution, but we have only briefly touched on the meaning and scope of the Religious Freedom Restoration Act, which is at the very core of the *Hobby Lobby* case. Can you explain RFRA and its significance here?

Shapiro: Sure. We need to back up a bit first to get some historical context. Through most of American history, religious objectors only got relief if the law explicitly provided it to them. For example, Quakers were historically exempt from the military draft. In the 1960s, beginning with the 1963 case of *Sherbert v. Verner*, the Supreme Court began recognizing constitutionally required exemptions. That experiment only lasted until the Supreme Court's 1990 ruling *Employment Division v. Smith*, which was written by Justice Scalia over a dissent by Justices Blackmun, Brennan, and Marshall. *Smith* upheld the constitutionality of generally applicable laws that burdened religion so long as they didn't specifically discriminate against religious people. If objectors wanted an exemption, they would have to seek it from the legislature.

Criticism of the decision came from all sides; nobody on any part of the political spectrum was too pleased with the new rule regarding religious (non-)accommodation. Accordingly, Congress passed RFRA, which created a presumptive statutory exemption from generally applicable laws, subject to the government's showing that the burden it imposed on believers was "the least restrictive means of furthering [a] compelling governmental interest." It's strange to imagine two decades hence, but RFRA passed the House unanimously and by a vote of 97–3 in the Senate. Two of its lead sponsors were Rep. Chuck Schumer (D-NY) and Sen. Ted Kennedy (D-MA)—not exactly conservative zealots. So an essentially unanimous Congress passed a law that effectively reversed a Supreme Court ruling whose dissenters were the three most liberal justices. This is the law that Hobby Lobby and others have invoked to challenge Obamacare's contraceptive mandate!

Although there was a lot of emotion surrounding RFRA when it passed, and a lot of emotion surrounding its application now, it's really a simple law. As I mentioned earlier, when someone makes a RFRA claim, courts look first at whether the government action at issue imposes a "substantial burden" on religious exercise. If it does, then the government must show that it nevertheless is pursuing a "compelling interest" and uses the "least restrictive means" of serving that interest. That's it.

DOI: 10.1057/9781137479709.0005

Gans: Let me make a couple of points in response. I agree with Ilya's summary of RFRA, but I would add that the whole point of the RFRA was to restore the body of pre-*Smith* law, not to establish some a regime presumptively mandating religious exemptions. Pre-*Smith*, most claims for religious exemptions were rejected. A few succeeded—mostly in rulings such as *Sherbert v. Verner* and others concerning the application of state unemployment compensation laws to devout individuals—but most were rejected, often by wide majorities of the Court. Out of a total of 18 free exercise cases that reached the Court, claims for religious exemptions were rejected in 13 of them.[39]

Second, and most important, under pre-*Smith* law, no commercial, profit-making business entity or individual business owner—let alone a secular, for-profit corporation such as Hobby Lobby—ever succeeded in obtaining a religious exemption from neutral, generally applicable business regulation. The history of those claims, as we have discussed, was one of total failure. In the most important of those cases—the *Lee* case which we discussed earlier—the justices unanimously recognized that granting a religious exemption would improperly extinguish the rights of employees. In that case, the Court refused to grant an exemption to an Amish business owner from having to make Social Security payments on behalf of his employees even though the government could have picked up the tab, concluding that to do so would impose the employer's religious beliefs on the employees, who have their own deeply held convictions. These fundamental principles continue to apply under RFRA.

Shapiro: Okay, but let's just remember that this case is being litigated under RFRA, that it's not a pure First Amendment Free Exercise Clause case. And that's why I think it's much easier than it might look otherwise, because RFRA is pretty clear in terms of its requirements. Yes—without RFRA, under *Employment Division v. Smith*, it's a whole new ballgame. To continue that metaphor, it would be a jump ball under the First Amendment. I'm of two minds on *Smith*, but ultimately, because this is a case of statutory interpretation, there's a lot less going on than people might otherwise think.

Gans: Ilya's certainly right about the centrality of RFRA to *Hobby Lobby*, but the whole point of the RFRA was to restore the pre-*Smith* law. And, as I said, part of the problem for Hobby Lobby is that the pre-*Smith* law was a total failure regarding claims by businesses, corporations, or business owners, to get religious exemptions from generally applicable laws.

DOI: 10.1057/9781137479709.0005

Rosen: Great, let me have some audience questions.

Audience #1: I wanted your opinion first on the issue of free speech. This strikes me as very different from a speech case. If I don't want to listen to what you're saying, there's no problem with my turning you off or tuning you out, but if a corporation has decided not to fund contraception and I work for that company, that corporate choice now offends my individual rights. I'm forced to spend money to get coverage that you're giving me as an employer. So it seems to me that the fundamental issue here is, when the employer exercises its rights, what happens when that violates my rights as an employee?

Rosen: Great question. David?

Gans: I think that hits the nail on the head. That's why I've made the point over and over again, as Ilya said, that Hobby Lobby's claim would impose the owners' religious beliefs on their employees and deny them the important federal rights the Affordable Care Act provides in order to ensure that women and their families can obtain the full range of FDA-approved contraceptives. I don't think it's an answer to say, well, they can buy it elsewhere. The whole point of the Affordable Care Act in this area is that historically insurance companies wouldn't cover contraceptives for women on the same basis as prescription coverage for men. Accordingly, the Act requires that employer-sponsored health plans provide contraceptive coverage.

Hobby Lobby's claim that it is entitled to a religious exemption from laws that protect the rights of its employees is extremely troubling, and raises the host of hypotheticals that I mentioned, that Jeff mentioned, and that Judge Rovner in the Seventh Circuit mentioned. Their claim is very much like the one in the *Lee* case we discussed earlier, in which the Amish owners sued to obtain a religious exemption from federal Social Security because it offended their religious beliefs. And the Court unanimously rejected the claim because giving the Amish an exemption would mean imposing their beliefs and denying the employees important rights provided by federal law. It's the same analysis here. And actually, *Hobby Lobby* is an even harder case because it's not an individual employer, but a corporation that wants to be treated as an individual for some purposes but also be treated as a corporation when it comes to all the special privileges that go with corporate status.

DOI: 10.1057/9781137479709.0005

Shapiro: What we're missing here is the prong in our law—in RFRA—that says plainly that if the government has a less offensive way of achieving the same goal, it has to pursue that. And here, it's very easy for the government to achieve the same goal in a different way. If the goal is to get people free contraceptives, the government could provide a tax credit; it could set up free clinics; it could even regulate insurance companies towards this end rather than employers; there are an infinite number of ways that the government could achieve the exact same goal without infringing on civil liberties. And so ultimately, on the merits—setting aside whether it's the corporate right or whether individuals acting through a corporate form have the right—that's why ultimately under RFRA (which, again passed near-unanimously in a bipartisanship that seems alien today) that's the standard. Social Security or taxation can't meet that standard; there's no way to achieve the same kind of general level of taxation without having everyone in it. It would be chaos. But there are plenty of other ways of getting people free contraceptives—assuming that's a compelling government interest in the first place.

Rosen: Wonderful. Next question. Yes, sir?

Audience #2: A corporation is a voluntary association, as are many organizations. In a voluntary association, one recourse is always to resign, to leave the association. Now, if a corporation requires an employee or any organization requires a participant to do something which is legal but the participant feels is immoral, that person has the right to leave that voluntary organization. On the other hand, if the government requires a voluntary organization to do something that its members regard as immoral, they, again, have a right to resign from that organization. So it seems to me that a corporation cannot reject a government mandate, since the participants always have the right to leave. The owners of Hobby Lobby have a right to sell off their business, in other words. To me, that supports the argument that the corporation or any voluntary organization does *not* have the rights of individuals, because that option to resign is always there.

Rosen: Ilya, why don't you start with that?

Shapiro: Under RFRA, the question with any law or government action where there's a religious objection is, "Is this a substantial burden?" In your example, sure they could close up shop, sell it off, but that would be a pretty substantial burden. They like what they're doing; they've

DOI: 10.1057/9781137479709.0005

built it, they've made it their life's work to provide this craft store emporium while promoting their vision of the good life. And to say that, "well, you can just leave, you can stop that activity," that burdens them immensely; it's no different, really than the choice of whether to act against their beliefs or pay $1.3 million in daily fines. This is no better—and moreover it makes society poorer. There's the bakery in Oregon which had to close down because it wouldn't be allowed not to create cakes for gay weddings, when there are lots of bakeries in Oregon that would[40]—and the wedding photographer in Albuquerque, where there are more than 100 businesses that would love to work those jobs.[41] It's not like this is a public accommodation in the Jim Crow South, where if you don't force a change in business practices, there's nowhere for people to eat or stay overnight while traveling. So again, if there's this substantial burden, can the government achieve the same goal without imposing that burden? Giving the choice of violating your beliefs or going out of business is no choice at all—akin to the mugger asking your money or your life. Is there a narrower way of achieving the underlying goal? Yes, there is.

Rosen: Yes, right in front.

Audience #3: You've talked about this a little bit, but is there a distinction between a closely held, private corporation and one that's a public, stock-offering corporation, in this regard?

Rosen: It's a great question and I don't know the answer. Can you explain to us the difference between a closely held corporation and a publicly owned stock corporation?

Gans: Well, *Hobby Lobby* and *Conestoga Wood* both involve closely held corporations in which there is a single family that has a controlling power. In the *Hobby Lobby* case, it is the Green family; in *Contestoga Wood*, it is the Hahns. The difficulty is that when the Supreme Court gets down to the task of spelling out the rights of business corporations, they don't create protections only for the parties before the Court; they establish general rules that will apply to all like cases.

One thing to keep in mind is, even when you're dealing with the smallest unit, which would be a corporation with a single shareholder, the fundamental point of incorporating is to disassociate the individual from the company, to recognize that there's a separate legal entity with separate rights, duties, and obligations.[42] Of course, the main reason that business owners choose to incorporate is to avoid liability, which is one of the most important special privileges given to corporations. Thus, in practice, while these cases all obviously involve this fact scenario of closely held, non-public corporations, the Court has to reason more broadly about the rights of all business corporations. It's hard to give this right to Hobby Lobby, but not to IBM. The principle will be generally applicable and that's why our debate here has focused on the larger question of whether corporations, particularly secular, for-profit corporations, have religious free exercise rights.

Finally, if you look to the Supreme Court's body of precedents, the cases uniformly analyze the rights of corporations from a broad angle rather than focusing on the specific kind of corporation before the Court. That's true of *Citizens United*, which gave the right to spend unlimited sums of money to all corporations; it is also true of cases, like *Braswell v. United States*, which applied the rule that corporations do not have rights under the Self-Incrimination Clause to the case of a corporation with a single shareholder.

Rosen: Just briefly, Ilya, you talked about creating a test—would that be one?

Shapiro: No, I don't draw the line between public versus closely held, and I agree with David that the principle has to apply more broadly. In practice, it's going to be very rare for some big public company to assert these sorts of rights and that's perhaps why you haven't seen the Googles or anyone like that involved in RFRA cases. Chick-fil-A, I believe, is a public company, but its stores close on Sundays. I don't know what the owners of that company believe with respect to the contraceptive mandate, but in practice it would be very rare to have such a huge, publicly traded corporation that's able to maintain a religious mission or something like that—and perhaps that's why business owners who have a religious calling keep their companies closely held and don't go public. Perhaps that's an incentive or a disincentive in the law to maintain your corporation that way. In principle I don't think there's a distinction, but in practice, again, there would have to be some sort of test about control and who's being burdened and the size of the burden and all these different sorts of factors would necessarily operate differently for closely held than for public companies.

Rosen: Great. Towards the back.

DOI: 10.1057/9781137479709.0005

Audience #4: My question follows kind of on the same lines, but a step farther. How would your analysis change if, instead of an incorporated business, we were talking about a sole proprietorship? Equal in every other way, in size and line of work, but one that was run out of the owner's pocket rather than as a separate legal entity. Would he or she then be able to claim religious rights?

Gans: I think that case would be governed by the Court's past cases such as *Braunfeld* and *Lee*. In those cases, the Court held that business owners could claim the protection of the Free Exercise Clause, but refused to grant religious exemptions to the owners. In the *Lee* case, as we have mentioned, the Court relied specifically on the fact that the exemption would impose the owner's religious beliefs on his employees. With respect to RFRA, you have to recognize that the history even prior to *Smith* is a history of claims brought by business owners being rejected over and over again. I'm not sure of any case that won, certainly not in the Supreme Court. So, if you're just dealing with the claim of an individual owner, those would be governed by *Braunfeld*, *Lee*, and other relevant cases. *Braunfeld*, remember, was the 1961 case that upheld Sunday closing laws, rejecting the efforts of Jewish merchants to obtain a religious exemption from those laws. One of the points made by Chief Justice Warren, who wrote the lead opinion, was that "we are a cosmopolitan nation made up of people of almost every conceivable religious preference" and opening the door to a variety of religious exemptions would undermine the government's regulatory interest in a day of rest.

Shapiro: Chief Justice Warren's point may or may not be right, but notice that it doesn't depend on the legal form of the business. And I don't think it should.

Rosen: Ladies and gentlemen, you've just heard an extremely sophisticated, nuanced, and complex discussion not about political issues, but about constitutional issues. You recognize that, like all important constitutional issues, the answers here aren't easy. Stay tuned.

Notes

1   See 1 Annals of Congress, 1st Cong., 1st Sess. 766 (1789) (proposal to ensure that "the equal rights of conscience" shall not be infringed); James Madison, Memorial and Remonstrance Against Religious Assessments, *in* 2 *The Writings*

of James Madison 183, 184 (G. Hunt ed. 1901) ("The Religion then of every man must be left to the conviction and conscience of every man; and it is the right of every man to exercise it as these may dictate."); N.Y. Const. of 1777, art. XXXVIII (providing that "the free exercise of religion... shall forever hereafter be allowed within this State to all mankind"); N.H. Const. of 1784, pt. I, art. V ("Every individual has a natural and inalienable right to worship GOD according to the dictates of his own conscience, and reason."); Va. Declaration of Rights of 1776, § 16 ("[R]eligion... can be directed only by reason and conviction...; therefore, all men are equally entitled to the free exercise of religion, according to the dictates of conscience"). For further discussion, see Michael W. McConnell, The Origins and Historical Understanding of Free Exercise of Religion, 103 *Harv. L. Rev.* 1409, 1456–59 (1990).

2   *Trustees of Dartmouth College v. Woodward*, 17 U.S. (4 Wheat.) 518, 636–38 (1819) ("Charitable or public-spirited individuals, desirous of making permanent appropriations for charitable or other useful purposes, find it impossible to effect their design securely and certainly without an incorporating act.").

3   "Corporations receive constitutional protection, as Dartmouth College did, in order to protect the constitutional rights of the individuals behind the artificial entity." Adam Winkler, Corporations and the First Amendment: Examining the Health of Democracy: Corporate Personhood and the Rights of Corporate Speech, 30 *Seattle L. Rev.* 863, 864 (2007).

4   *See, e.g. Marshall v. Barlow's Inc.*, 436 U.S. 307 (1978).

5   *See, e.g. Chicago B. & Q. R. Co. v. City of Chicago*, 166 U.S. 226 (1897).

6   *Gilardi v. United States Dep't of Health and Human Servs.*, 733 F.3d 1208 (D.C. Cir. 2013).

7   *See Morton Salt*, 338 U.S. at 652.

8   366 U.S. 599 (1961).

9   *Id.* at 610; *McGowan v. Maryland*, 366 U.S. 420, 459–543 (1960) (opinion of Frankfurter, J.).

10   *Braunfeld*, 366 U.S. at 603–09.

11   374 U.S. 398 (1963).

12   494 U.S. 872 (1990).

13   *Thomas v. Review Bd. of the Indiana Emp. Sec. Div.*, 450 U.S. 707 (1981) (foundry employee who wouldn't work on military armaments for religious reasons entitled to unemployment benefits), *Hobbie v. Unemployment Appeals Comm'n*, 480 U.S. 136 (1987) (employee fired for not working on Sabbath had constitutional right to unemployment compensation from the government), and *Frazee v. Illinois Dept. of Emp. Sec.*, 489 U.S. 829 (1989) (same). Selling one's labor is of course more important to more people's lives than selling goods, but both are commercial activity.

DOI: 10.1057/9781137479709.0005

14   1 J. Cox & T. Hazen, *Treatise of the Law of Corporations* §4:1, p. 224 (3d ed. 2010); see 1A W. Fletcher, *Cyclopedia of the Law of Corporations* §102 (rev. ed. 2010).

15   *See* Brief of Cato Institute in *Burwell v. Hobby Lobby* (January 28, 2014), available at http://object.cato.org/sites/cato.org/files/pubs/pdf/hobby-lobby-filed-brief.pdf.

16   *Conestoga Wood Specialties Corp. v. Sec'y of the U.S. Dep't of Health & Human Servs.*, 724 F.3d 377, 398 n.14 (3d Cir. 2013) (Jordan, J., dissenting).

17   *Id.* at 400 (Jordan, J., dissenting).

18   *Braunfeld*, 366 U.S. at 607, 608 (opinion of Warren, J.).

19   455 U.S. 282 (1982).

20   *Id.* at 261 ("When followers of a particular sect enter into commercial activity as a matter of choice, the limits they accept on their own conduct as a matter of conscience and faith are not to be superimposed on statutory schemes which are binding on others in that activity. Granting an exemption from social security taxes to an employer operates to impose the employer's religious faith on the employees.").

21   *See United States v. White*, 322 U.S. 694, 698 (1944) (explaining that the Self-Incrimination Clause "grows out of the high sentiment and regard of our jurisprudence for conducting criminal trials and investigatory proceedings on a plane of dignity, humanity and impartiality"). In fact, the origins of the rights against compelled self-incrimination and the right to religious free exercise are closely linked. *See* Akhil Reed Amar, *The Bill of Rights: Creation and Reconstruction* 82–83 (1998); William Stuntz, The Substantive Origins of Criminal Procedure, 105 *Yale L.J.* 393, 411–12 (1995) (explaining that "the privilege entered the law in response to practices that were troubling... because of the crimes being prosecuted" including "crimes of religious belief"). As Prof. Stuntz explained, critics of compelled oaths viewed them as violations of freedom of conscience: "put[ting] the conscience uppon [sic] the racke." *Id.* at 412.

22   *Braswell*, 487 U.S. at 110.

23   *Id.*

24   *See, e.g. First National Bank of Boston v. Bellotti*, 435 U.S. 765 (1978). Indeed, the Court in *Citizens United* took pains to rely on this earlier precedent, citing extensively from *Bellotti* and other cases. *Citizens United*, 558 U.S. at 899–900 (string citing cases).

25   *Conestoga Wood*, 724 F.3d at 389.

26   38 U.S. (13 Pet.) 519 (1839).

27   *Id.* at 586–87.

28   *FCC v. AT & T, Inc.*, 131 S. Ct. 1177, 1185 (2011).

29   *Hosanna-Tabor Evangelical Lutheran Church and School v. EEOC*, 132 S. Ct. 694 (2012).

30 *See* David H. Gans, Discrimination, Inc., *Constitution Daily* (February 28, 2014), http://blog.constitutioncenter.org/2014/02/discrimination-inc/.

31 *Id.* at 706.

32 1 William Blackstone, *Commentaries on the Law of England* *470 (1768) (observing the "division of corporations…into ecclesiastical and lay. Ecclesiastical corporations are where the members that compose it are entirely spiritual persons…. These are erected for furtherance of religion, and perpetuating the rights of the church").

33 *See* John Locke, A Letter Concerning Toleration 28 (1689) (James H. Tully ed. 1983) (describing a church as a "voluntary society of men, joining together of their own accord, in order to the public worshipping of God, in such manner as they judge acceptable to him, and effectual to the salvation of their souls"); *see also* Douglas Laycock, Towards a General Theory of the Religion Clauses: The Case of Church Labor Relations and the Right to Church Autonomy, 81 *Colum. L. Rev.* 1373, 1389 (1981) ("Religion includes important communal elements for most believers. They exercise religion through religious organizations, and these organizations must be protected by the [Free Exercise] Clause.").

34 42 U.S.C. § 2000e-1.

35 *Korte v. Sebelius*, 735 F.3d 654, 689 (7th Cir. 2013) (Rovner, J., dissenting).

36 *Id.* at 689–93 (Rovner, J., dissenting).

37 *See, e.g. Adams v. Commissioner of Internal Revenue*, 170 F.3d 173, 178 (3d Cir. 1999) (collecting cases).

38 *See generally* Eugene Volokh, Sebelius v. Hobby Lobby: *Corporate Rights and Religious Liberties* (2014).

39 *See* James E. Ryan, Note, Smith and the Religious Freedom Restoration Act: An Iconoclastic Assessment, 78 *Va. L. Rev.* 1407, 1458 (1992).

40 See Evan Sernoffsky, Gresham Bakery That Denied Same-Sex Wedding Cake Closes, KGW.com (September 1, 2013), available at http://www.kgw.com/home/Gresham-bakery-that-denied-same-sex-wedding-cake-closes--222004711.html.

41 *See* Adam Liptak, Weighing Free Speech in Refusal to Photograph Lesbian Couple's Ceremony, *N.Y. Times* (November 18, 2013), available at http://www.nytimes.com/2013/11/19/us/weighing-free-speech-in-refusal-to-photograph-ceremony.html.

42 This is a point the Supreme Court has recognized many times. *See, e.g. Cedric Kushner Promotions, Ltd. v. King,* 533 U.S. 158, 163 (2001); *Domino's Pizza, Inc. v. McDonald,* 546 U.S. 470, 477 (2006).

DOI: 10.1057/9781137479709.0005

3

The Broader Implications of *Hobby Lobby*: Is There a Slippery Slope?

Abstract: *This chapter assesses the oral arguments in* Hobby Lobby *and extrapolates the consequences of an eventual ruling. The authors agreed that standing—whether plaintiffs could properly raise their religious liberty claim (as corporations or individuals)—didn't interest the Supreme Court very much. Instead, the debate centered on the merits of the corporation's claim, the consequences of ruling for plaintiffs, how broad that ruling would be, and whether it would open the door to new religious-exemption claims. Gans argued that it would be unprecedented to recognize an exemption that extinguished the rights of employees, while Shapiro thought that RFRA made the case simpler because the government could accomplish its goal through other means. Both identified Justice Kennedy as a key player.*

Keywords: access to contraceptives; consequences; free exercise; Hobby Lobby; Justice Kennedy; religious exemptions; rights of employees; Supreme Court

Gans, David H., and Ilya Shapiro. *Religious Liberties for Corporations?: Hobby Lobby, the Affordable Care Act, and the Constitution.* New York: Palgrave Macmillan, 2014. DOI: 10.1057/9781137479709.0006.

DOI: 10.1057/9781137479709.0006

Jeffrey Rosen: Today[1] we're going to discuss one of the most hotly contested Supreme Court cases of the term, the *Hobby Lobby* case, as well as a related case called *Conestoga Wood*. Ilya and David, both of you were at the Court for the argument. First, let me ask you, Ilya, what surprising details or exchanges struck you in the courtroom?

Ilya Shapiro: Well, I was surprised that the government didn't spend that much time—and the Court didn't seem that interested in hearing the government's argument—on standing, the question of whether a corporation can raise the religious liberty claim or rather, is it the individuals behind it that have standing to raise the claim? The Court seemed to bypass these threshold issues, instead wanting to get directly into the heart of the argument over whether the contraceptive mandate illegally violated religious liberty under RFRA.

Rosen: Very interesting. David, you also were in the courtroom. What surprised you?

Gans: After the argument, this case tees up what may be the most important case on the meaning of the guarantee of the free exercise of religion that the Court has decided in decades. The fundamental question is whether the Court's conservatives will extend free exercise rights to secular businesses and allow them to extinguish the rights of their employees. I think Ilya is right that there was perhaps less focus on the question of whether corporations have free exercise rights. Justice Ruth Bader Ginsburg and Justice Sonia Sotomayor pressed Paul Clement, Hobby Lobby's counsel, to explain how corporations exercise religion, but the real issue was whether the rights of employees count at all. Justice Anthony Kennedy was alone among the conservative justices in suggesting that they do deserve some weight in the balance. But the other conservative justices seemed to suggest that employers should be entitled to a broad range of religious exemptions that would override the rights of employees. That would allow the owners of secular, for-profit corporations, like Hobby Lobby, to impose their religious views on their employees and to deny them their federal rights. I think that would be a very troubling result that would turn religious liberty on its head, effectively allowing employers to maintain a religious orthodoxy in the workplace.

Justice Elena Kagan, Justice Sotomayor, and Justice Ginsburg all pushed Paul Clement for a limiting principle. What would you do about cases

DOI: 10.1057/9781137479709.0006

where an employer objects on religious grounds to a blood transfusion or to vaccinations or medications that are made with pork products? Clement really had no answer. He had no limiting principle. One of the interesting things is that, unlike in the constitutional challenge to the Affordable Care Act two years ago,[2] here there was the potential of a very far reaching precedent but no real answer from conservative justices of where this would stop.

Rosen: Let's disaggregate the arguments. Let's start with this standing question, and that's a technical way of saying: does a corporation have standing to bring a lawsuit, claiming that its own religious rights were infringed? Justice Sotomayor asked Paul Clement, "How does a corporation exercise religion? I mean I know how it speaks, and we have, according to our jurisprudence, 200 years of corporations speaking in its own interests. But where are the cases that show corporation exercises religion?" Ilya, what was Paul Clement's response to Justice Sotomayor's question and what generally did you sense the conservative justices concluding about this question of whether corporations have standing to bring these suits?

Shapiro: I think we have to distinguish the exercise of religion and worshipping. Clearly, corporations don't worship. They don't have souls. They don't get down on their knees and pray. And Paul Clement talked about how the corporation was used, or how it was *operationalized*, by the people who own and run it in a way that comports with their particular faith, in terms of closing on Sundays, not selling shot glasses, and all the rest of it. One of the plaintiffs is a Christian bookstore called Mardel, even more explicitly religious in that sense. And then, the conservative justices had even more to say on that. Chief Justice John Roberts and Justice Samuel Alito, in questioning Solicitor General Verrilli, discussed how we have precedent that for-profit enterprises—not necessarily corporations—have religious rights. The kosher butcher is the prototypical one that came up again and again. And corporate entities can have a religious mission as well, such as religious organizations that are non-profit. So if it's not the corporate/non-corporate line or for-profit/non-profit line that's decisive, then how does congealing the two in the context of a for-profit corporation somehow make the difference? Solicitor General Verrilli didn't have a convincing answer. As a result, he had to fall back on the merits of the government's argument that it has a compelling interest that overcomes the burden that the mandate places, whether it be on the

DOI: 10.1057/9781137479709.0006

corporation or on its owners, in terms of the mandate to insure certain types of devices and medicines that they find religiously offensive—or to pay the astronomical fines if they don't comply.

Rosen: David, tell us about the standing argument. You filed a brief saying that never before in more than 200 years has the Court recognized corporations as persons for free exercise purposes. And, yet in the argument, as Ilya suggested, the Court's conservative justices, and perhaps others, did seem to assume that the corporations have religious free exercise rights. What was the best argument on the other side that they were resisting and what were the liberal justices saying about this?

David H. Gans: The key argument we heard in the Court—and this was alluded to by Justices Sotomayor and Ginsburg—was that this is a right that secular for-profit corporations have never claimed to possess in over two centuries. If you look at the Constitution's text and history and other Founding-era statements on religious liberty that we discussed previously, the right to free exercise of religion has always been a personal individual right that protects freedom of conscience and human dignity. It does not meaningfully apply to secular, for-profit corporations, like these, who employ persons of all religious faiths. Certainly, the owners have deeply held religious beliefs, but there's a fundamental difference between the owners and Hobby Lobby. In a sense, what Hobby Lobby wants is to have its cake and eat it too—to get all the special privileges of corporate status, including limited liability, so that when they're sued, the owners aren't on the hook. But when it comes to the money that the corporation spends, Hobby Lobby wants that money to be treated as the owners' money. There's a fundamental inconsistency there. If you take the Constitution's text and history seriously—as the justices should—there is no basis for holding that secular for-profit corporations have free exercise rights. In fact, there's always been a distinction between religious organizations, where people come together to exercise religion communally, and for-profit corporations, even in these cases where they are run by devout individuals. It's a sign of how far the Roberts Court has taken the idea of corporate personhood that the Court's five conservative justices breezed over these issues.

Rosen: Ilya, I want to have one more beat on the standing question. Were you surprised that it was not primarily conducted in constitutional terms? In a dissent filed in the Tenth Circuit in the *Hobby Lobby* case, Chief Judge Mary Beck Briscoe said the ruling was "nothing short of a

DOI: 10.1057/9781137479709.0006

radical revision of First Amendment law, as well as the law of corpora-tions" to recognize corporations as persons for religious purposes.[4] But the argument here seemed to focus more on the question of whether corporations were persons exercising religion under the Religious Freedom Restoration Act. There were technical questions of whether the religious people had to own 51 percent of the shares. The solicitor general was insisting that the past cases where Jewish business owners sought exemptions from Sabbath closing laws involved them as individuals, not as corporations. Lead us through why the question of corporate person-hood seemed to be narrower than the dissent in the Tenth Circuit had suggested.

Shapiro: That actually dovetails nicely with the brief that I filed on behalf of Cato. This is really an academic question. It might be interesting to know who is asserting the right of the corporation and whether it's the directors or the officers or the shareholders or whatever the case may be. Or is it the individuals exercising and asserting their own rights, through the corporate form or otherwise? Is it different in a closely held versus a public Fortune 500 company? Does it even matter for this case? Chief Justice Roberts at one point said that it's very unlikely for Exxon to do something like this, but that you'd end up looking to state corporate law about whether the corporation is actually acting in a religious way.[5] That would be unlikely to come up, but still, as a matter of first principles, I don't think people check their religious rights, no less than other types of rights—whether you're talking about the right to be free from unreason-able search and seizure or the right to participate in political speech or anything else—when they associate together, whether that be in the cor-porate form or any other. And the IRS tax treatment of for-profit versus non-profit corporations doesn't really matter.

At the end of the day, most of the justices recognized that this has to stand or fall on the RFRA analysis—and that also came up, that if the Court can decide this on the statutory question rather than going to the constitutional one, it will. There's a way for the Court to do that because the Dictionary Act, which applies to RFRA, defines personhood quite broadly,[6] and again, because the people who are operating these particu-lar companies, whether Hobby Lobby, Mardel bookstore, or Conestoga Wood, the Mennonite wood- and lumber-producing company, do operate their companies in a religious manner. That's why the standing question ultimately fell away and the justices were interested in really

DOI: 10.1057/9781137479709.0006

seeing whether there really was any harm to third parties, say, and other merits questions under RFRA. The employees would no longer be getting the contraceptives paid for. They still have access, of course, but they wouldn't have them paid for by the employer. Is that significant? Is that a compelling interest for the government to overcome the burden they're imposing on their religious beliefs? That sort of thing. So, I don't think it would be a radical extension or expansion of any rights if the Court were to rule in favor of the plaintiffs. As many have said, and as we've discussed before here at the National Constitution Center, corporate rights have existed for a long, long time. This isn't something new from *Citizens United* or other cases in the modern era. In this context, again, it's not that corporations are praying on their knees or anything like that, but they are operated by the people through their religious faith. The claims can be raised and need to be adjudicated on their merits.

Rosen: David, as Ilya suggests, Chief Justice Roberts did seem interested in a narrower ruling that might hold that closely held corporations have the ability to bring suit under RFRA, tabling the question of whether other, larger or public corporations have those rights, and not reaching the constitutional question of whether corporations are persons for First Amendment purposes. If he could persuade the majority of the Court to go along with that compromise, including perhaps Justice Breyer, would that be a radical revision of current law or would it be a modest ruling that you could live with?

Gans: It would be a radical revision of free exercise law. One of the biggest developments to come out of oral argument was that Chief Justice Roberts and the other conservative justices viewed RFRA as a break from prior First Amendment law and an occasion to revamp and create a new broad right for secular businesses to have religious exemptions that would extinguish the rights of their employees. When Solicitor General Verrilli began his argument by quoting Justice Jackson's 1944 statement from *Prince v. Massachusetts* that limitations on religious freedom kick in when they "collide with the liberty of others,"[7] Chief Justice Roberts snapped back, "That's a statement that's inconsistent with RFRA, isn't it? The whole point of RFRA is that Congress wanted to provide exceptions for the religious views of particular—including proprietors, individuals."[8] His view and that of a number of the other conservative justices was that the rights of the employees don't count at all and that RFRA supports granting a host of religious exemptions that would extinguish those

DOI: 10.1057/9781137479709.0006

rights. That's directly contrary to the basic First Amendment law that was in play in the 1980s, well before *Employment Division v. Smith* changed everything. That's the body of free exercise law that was supposed to be restored by RFRA, and it seems that the Court's conservative justices are seeking not to restore, but instead, to remake free exercise principles to grant a wide swath of religious exemptions.

To be sure, Chief Justice Roberts was focused in exploring ways to decide Hobby Lobby's case, and leave other questions—such as the rights of publicly held corporations like Google and others—for another day.[9] He recognized, as Ilya has pointed out, that publicly traded corporations might not even claim religious free exercise rights. In this regard, the contrast to the blockbuster challenge to the Affordable Care Act decided by the Supreme Court in 2010 is remarkable. When that case was debated, the conservative justices didn't say, "well, no one's going to pass the broccoli mandate." They asked for a limiting principle. Here the conservative bloc on the Court had no limiting principle, and Paul Clement offered no assistance in how to limit a ruling that secular businesses have the right to religious exemptions that extinguish the rights of their employees. This key issue, as I mentioned, was pressed by Justice Kagan, by Justice Sotomayor, and by Justice Ginsburg, and there really was no answer to their concerns that a ruling in favor of Hobby Lobby would prove difficult to cabin.

In short, the Court's conservatives seemed inclined to hold that secular, for-profit corporations were entitled to religious exemptions that would allow them to impose their religious beliefs on their employees. And, it was only Justice Kennedy who recognized the differences between a religious organization, where all members share a certain faith, and a secular business, where the "employee may not agree with the...religious beliefs of the employer."[10] In that setting, Justice Kennedy appeared to recognize that it was unacceptable to permit employers' religious beliefs to act as a "trump," allowing "the employer to put the employee in a disadvantageous position."[11]

The question is what will come of Justice Kennedy's questions as he thinks deeply about this case, and the justices begin the process of writing a decision. Coming out of argument, what we are seeing is the making of a very broad precedent that would create a body of free exercise law that really has no roots in anything the Supreme Court has ever done. Even before RFRA, we had a body of free exercise law that allowed an

DOI: 10.1057/9781137479709.0006

individual or a religious organization to obtain a religious exemption in some circumstances, but most of the time, those claims failed. In almost 20 Supreme Court cases, only a handful of claims prevailed, and those were almost all in the context of unemployment compensation. It seems, that in the hands of the conservative justices, now we're going to have a body of law that grants a broad range of religious exemptions.

Shapiro: Okay, that's just not true. I'm going to start pushing back on this. First of all, the limiting principle issue is an issue when we're dealing with government powers because those are limited and finite. Rights, however, are infinite, and they're only cabined when the government has a compelling reason to do so because you're violating other people's rights or something equally primal. The structure of RFRA isn't that a religious objection always trumps. This is the same mischaracterization of Arizona's Religious Freedom Restoration Act introduced earlier this month, known as SB 1062.[12] It's not just that I raise my religious objection, whatever it may be to whatever law, and that's it, I win. That's not at all the way it works. You raise your objection, and then courts are to determine whether, first of all, that's a sincerely held belief—and Paul Clement talked about the many cases where they'll reject the claims, for example, of people who are arrested for marijuana-related crimes and then say that they're members of the Church of Marijuana.[13] That's obviously pretextual. So then, if there *is* a sincere belief, is there a substantial burden on that belief? You don't just look at whether it's something essential to the religion, but is it burdening a religious belief substantially? And then that's still not the end of the story. Then courts look at (1) whether nevertheless the government has a compelling interest to impose that burden and (2) whether it has narrowly tailored its action, that is, that it's used the "least restrictive means" to accomplish its goal. In other words, is this the only way of achieving that compelling interest? That's the standard that RFRA puts into place.

And so here it would be a different case if Hobby Lobby wanted an exemption from, say, employment discrimination laws and only wanted to hire Christians or only wanted to hire people who didn't use contraceptives. This is not that case. All that the Greens (the owners of Hobby Lobby) and the Hahns (the owners of Conestoga) are asserting is that it burdens them to be forced to use their own money to pay for things that violate their religious beliefs. That's where the debate is. Are there possible alternatives, such as a public health clinic, or a tax credit for

DOI: 10.1057/9781137479709.0006

the employees, or structuring the financial transaction in a different way? Are those possible, and has the government articulated a strong enough compelling interest? In the courts below, where the government lost, it did so because the courts said that the interests asserted—"gender equality" and "public health"—are too broad, not articulated specifically enough.[14] I mean, it's like saying that we have an interest in "good public policy." It's simply not enough.

Finally, not as to the limiting principles, but as to the parade of horribles—because, again, when you're talking about rights, there is no limiting principle—RFRA contemplates going in a case-by-case manner. We're supposed to trust the judiciary. That's how Congress wrote the text, to go through these cases and, as Paul Clement said, separate the goats from the sheep.[15] So if you have an objection to blood transfusions or vaccines, that might approach the type of case, like *United States v. Lee*, the Amish challenge to paying Social Security taxes for his employees, which the Supreme Court rejected because that's a generalized law that would fall apart if you allowed exemptions. With vaccines there's a similar concern for herd immunity. Here, the kinds of third-party or public burdens associated with allowing an exemption are much less. But, again, it's a case-by-case determination. You can't just say that with the Court's ruling in *Hobby Lobby*, whichever way it goes, we'll know how every future court will rule on every future religious objection in the RFRA context.

Rosen: The arguments on the merits are well-joined and well-described. I want to have one more round on them. David, the liberal justices were suggesting that Congress could never have intended to increase the standard of scrutiny with RFRA and explicitly rejected an attempt to create an exemption for religiously motivated business owners. More broadly, liberal commentators have been focusing on Justice Scalia, who wrote the opinion in *Employment Division v. Smith* that RFRA overturned and suggested if he were true to his vision of the First Amendment, he would reject the higher standard of scrutiny. Tell us about that argument, about Scalia's position, and basically, what you think RFRA was intended to do.

Gans: RFRA was designed to restore the balanced jurisprudence that characterized free exercise law from 1963 (*Sherbert v. Verner*) until 1990 (*Smith*). Congress's view was that Justice Scalia's ruling in *Smith*, which was that the First Amendment required no religious exemptions, was wrong. Instead, the near-unanimous view was that sometimes religious exemptions should carry the day and sometimes they shouldn't. And if you look at that body of law, most of the time they were rejected. Out of 18 Supreme Court cases decided from 1963 to 1990, claims for religious exemptions lost in 13. But the view that we heard from Justice Scalia, Chief Justice Roberts, and others at the *Hobby Lobby* argument was, in essence, that the rights of employees don't count. That's troubling because it is not only the rights of the owners of a company that are at stake here. There are the rights of employees as well, and employees shouldn't have to check their personal liberty and their human dignity at the workplace door when they enter.

Ilya has said that the way that the government has described its interest here is too broad, too vague, and that it is akin to a nebulous interest in "good public policy." That's an unjustified characterization. What is at issue in Hobby Lobby is the Affordable Care Act's goal of ensuring that hardworking women have access to the full range of FDA-approved contraceptives. Right now, the IUD—the most effective *and most expensive* contraceptive—is one of the ones that Hobby Lobby wants to refuse to cover.[16] And without insurance coverage, women won't obtain it.

The question at the heart of the case is whether Hobby Lobby should have a free exercise right under RFRA to override and extinguish the rights of employees protected by federal law and impose their own religious beliefs on people who do not share those beliefs and have fundamental rights to personal liberty and human dignity that deserve equal respect. Ilya's argument allows the rights of those employees to be trampled on. When he says that the government's interest is just "good public policy," that means that all the other requirements that are in the Affordable Care Act—such as cancer screening or immunizations—would not be compelling either under Ilya's formulation. I don't know where Ilya's definition of compelling comes from, but to me, protecting public health and ensuring equal access to health care is an interest of the highest order, not one that's unduly vague. Interests of this sort have been widely accepted by the courts for years.[17]

Rosen: Ilya, your response, and also your thoughts on why it wouldn't be inconsistent for Justice Scalia to rule in favor of Hobby Lobby, given how he voted in *Smith*.

Shapiro: The fundamental point is that nobody is denying access. This is not a case about whether women have the right to access contraceptives, or abortion, or any other types of legal procedures, products, or devices. It's the issue of whether the employer can be forced to pay for those things. The protestors outside the Court yesterday, the pro-government protestors, were saying "get my boss out of my business." Well, bosses don't want to be in the birth control business. If it's so important, if it's so compelling that women are not—because of cost or otherwise—getting the birth control they need, then set up your clinic under Title X of the Public Health Act, or provide tax credits, or throw in some other weird provision into Obamacare (and then illegally delay it a few times because it's not working or for some political reason).

And by the way, I fully support birth control and personally don't object to any of these things that Hobby Lobby objects to. But there are lots of ways to accomplish whatever the important goal here is. My point about the vague compelling interest isn't that public health isn't important. Of course it is, but if asserting "public health" was enough, then the government would have plenary power to violate any fundamental rights in its name—and believe me, lawyers will be able to argue that any policy is necessary for public health. No, the way RFRA works, in terms of how a compelling interest test operates, courts simply do not accept broad notions of "good policy" or "equality" or "motherhood and apple pie and 'murica." And that's why Scalia can rule for Hobby Lobby without backpedaling from his own opinion in *Smith*.

This is a statutory case. It's going to be decided on RFRA and therefore Scalia, in interpreting RFRA, can very easily say that the First Amendment only provides a certain level of protection for religious free exercise but Congress put in a higher level. He'd be enforcing the statute, not changing his mind on the constitutional question.

Rosen: Brief closing thoughts. How will Justice Kennedy vote? As both of you have noted, he expressed sympathy for the rights of employees, but also was concerned that employers might be forced to fund abortions over their objections. Of course, Kennedy wrote the opinion in 1997 in *City of Boerne v. Flores*, that struck down RFRA with respect to state and local governments as exceeding Congress' power to enforce the 14th Amendment.[18] And he also wrote the *Citizens United* opinion about corporations having First Amendment rights regarding political speech. So he's pulled in a bunch of different directions. David, how do you expect he might resolve them?

Gans: Judging by Justice Kennedy's questions towards the close of the argument, it did not seem that he would be convinced by the argument that corporations don't have free exercise rights. So instead I expect him to take the position—whether he writes an opinion or joins it—if he's true to RFRA and the body of law that RFRA was designed to restore, that what the Court said in *Lee* still holds. That is, an employer doesn't get a religious exemption that would allow him to impose his religious beliefs on his employees. Justice Kennedy expressed concern that there were a number of exemptions in the Affordable Care Act and its implementing regulations, but if you look throughout the body of the Court's free exercise jurisprudence, the laws that the Court has let stand were honeycombed with exceptions. If you look at other laws that came up, such as Title VII's prohibition against employment discrimination, those also have exemptions for small employers and religious employers. If you look at the Americans with Disabilities Act (ADA), that landmark act provided for a lengthy phase-in. The ADA's anti-discrimination provisions did not kick in immediately; other provisions were subject to an even long period of delay. Justice Kennedy should recognize —and I think it is consistent with his libertarian jurisprudence—that the Affordable Care Act's contraceptive mandate is designed to ensure that hardworking women can protect their health and control their reproductive lives, and that Hobby Lobby shouldn't get a religious exemption from its requirements.

Rosen: Great. Last word to you, Ilya. Please channel Justice Kennedy.

Shapiro: That's even harder to predict than the Court as a whole! (Indeed, I have a Justice Kennedy bobblehead in my office that I use as a magic 8-ball, seeing whether he nods or shakes his head when I ask him a question.) If I had to make an educated guess, I'd say that he obviously gets past the standing issue and focuses on the third-party burdens. I think he was probably troubled by the issue of corporations or private individuals being forced to pay for abortions. I think he can avoid the parade of horribles and rule narrowly in a way that Chief Justice Roberts will certainly like. He'll apply the very basic RFRA rubric that I've gone through before. Ultimately this case becomes much ado about not very much in the greater public health context—but it's certainly very important for religious liberty.

Rosen: Great. Well, we look forward to seeing whether your predictions were correct when the case is decided, and bringing both of you together to discuss it once the opinion is issued.

DOI: 10.1057/9781137479709.0006

Notes

1   This chapter is based on a National Constitution Center podcast that was recorded on March 26, 2014, soon after oral argument in the *Hobby Lobby* case.

2   *Nat'l Fed'n of Independent Business v. Sebelius*, 132 S. Ct. 256 (2012).

3   Transcript of Oral Argument at 17–18, available at http://www.supremecourt. gov/oral_arguments/argument_transcripts/13-354_3ebh.pdf.

4   *Hobby Lobby Stores, Inc. v. Sebelius*, 723 F.3d 1114, 1172 (10th Cir. 2013) (en banc) (Briscoe, C.J., concurring in part and dissenting in part).

5   Tr. of Oral Argument at 52, 53.

6   The Dictionary Act, which applies "unless the context indicates otherwise," provides that the word "'person'... include[s] corporations, associations, firms, partnerships, societies, and joint stock companies, as well as individuals." 1 U.S.C. § 1.

7   *Prince v. Massachusetts*, 321 U.S. 158, 177 (1944) (opinion of Jackson, J.).

8   Tr. of Oral Argument at 41.

9   *Id.* at 52.

10 *Id.* at 33.

11 *Id.*

12 Ilya Shapiro, *For Marriage Equality, Religious Liberty, and Freedom of Association*, Cato at Liberty (February 26, 2014), available at http://www.cato. org/blog/marriage-equality-religious-liberty-freedom-association.

13 Tr. of Oral Arg. at 20.

14 *See, e.g. Gilardi*, 733 F.3d at 1219–22.

15 Tr. of Oral Arg. at 14.

16 The IUD is 45 times more effective than oral contraceptives and 90 times more effective than male condoms. At the same time, IUDs are quite expensive, and often beyond reach for many women. Beginning use of IUD can cost a month's salary for a woman working full time at minimum wage. For discussion, see Brief of the Guttmacher Institute and Prof. Sarah Rosenbaum in *Burwell v. Hobby Lobby* (January 2014), available at http://www. americanbar.org/content/dam/aba/publications/supreme_court_preview/ briefs-v3/13-354-13-356_amcu_gi-psr.authcheckdam.pdf.

17 *See, e.g. Roberts v. United States Jaycees*, 468 U.S. 609 (1984) (gender equality); *Jacobson v. Massachusetts*, 197 U.S. 11 (1905) (public health).

18 521 U.S. 507 (1997).

DOI: 10.1057/9781137479709.0006

4
The Ruling: What Does It All Mean?

Abstract: *This chapter collects the authors' reactions to and analysis of the Supreme Court's ruling in favor of* Hobby Lobby *Shapiro thinks that the decision has been overblown, that it's a clear and correct application of statutory text. It's a win for religious liberty, but it's not a seminal Supreme Court moment. Moreover, Hobby Lobby's employees can still buy any contraceptives they want, while the government has many ways of providing them without cost. Gans disagrees, pointing out that for the first time, the Court recognized a corporate right to religious exercise—at the cost of women for whom it'll be harder to obtain certain contraceptives. In Gans's view, the ruling turns liberty on its head, allowing corporate owners to impose their beliefs on their employees.*

Keywords: contraceptives; corporate rights; Justice Alito; Justice Ginsburg; parade of horribles; religious liberty; RFRA; reproductive freedom; rights of employees

Gans, David H., and Ilya Shapiro. *Religious Liberties for Corporations?: Hobby Lobby, the Affordable Care Act, and the Constitution.* New York: Palgrave Macmillan, 2014. DOI: 10.1057/9781137479709.0007.

Jeffrey Rosen: Today[1] we discuss the most hotly contested Supreme Court decision of the term moments after it came down: the *Hobby Lobby* case involving the religious liberty of corporations. Ilya, the Court has come down decisively for your side. Why don't you describe what Justice Alito's opinion held and whether you were surprised by the breadth of his holding.

Ilya Shapiro: Sure, and thanks again for having me and David both discussing this important case throughout the term. I actually think that this is being made into a bigger deal than it should be. This was a statutory interpretation case. It wasn't about the scope of the First Amendment or balancing religious liberty against other important values or anything like that.

This was about an application of this statute, RFRA, the Religious Freedom Restoration Act, that was passed unanimously by the House and 97–3 by the Senate, signed by President Clinton in 1993, that said, very basically, that if the government passes a law that substantially burdens somebody's religious exercise, that person can file a claim in court and the government can still win if it can show that it has a compelling interest to nevertheless impose that burden and it has exercised the most narrow means of effecting that goal.

Here Justice Alito, writing for a five-justice majority, said first that at least closely held corporations can raise religious liberty claims[2]—the vote was actually 5–2 on that point, with Justices Breyer and Kagan not joining in this part of Justice Ginsburg's dissent—and second that the government hasn't shown to the Court's satisfaction that there are no alternatives to the requirement that employers provide, as part of their Obamacare-compliant health insurance policies, these four contraceptive methods that the plaintiffs object to on religious grounds.[3] Because there are alternatives available, or at least the government hasn't shown that there aren't, the challenge under RFRA succeeds.

Rosen: David, Ilya just characterized this as not a particularly big deal, but Justice Ginsburg in her passionate dissenting opinion called it "a decision of startling breadth."[4] Do you agree with Justice Ginsberg or Ilya? And tell us what you think the significance of this holding is.

David H. Gans: This case is a huge deal. I am surprised to hear Ilya back away from that. First of all, this is the first time in American law and history that the Supreme Court has ever held that a secular, for-profit

DOI: 10.1057/9781137479709.0007

corporation has religious free exercise rights. Here, we're dealing not with the interpretation of the Free Exercise Clause, but rather with the interpretation of RFRA, a statute designed to protect free exercise rights, as Ilya mentioned. But the fundamental question at issue is whether free exercise protections extend to secular, for-profit corporations. For the first time in history, in a bitterly divided opinion, the Court says yes. This is a hugely consequential statement.

Second, also for the first time in history, the Court ruled that a secular for-profit corporation is entitled to a religious exemption from general business regulation protecting the rights of employees. This, too, marks a decisive shift from long standing free exercise law. Prior to *Hobby Lobby*, the Supreme Court had consistently rejected claims by commercial businesses for a religious exemption from neutral, generally applicable business regulation. Justice Alito's 5–4 majority opinion broke wholly new ground in extending free exercise protections to secular, for-profit corporations and according them religious exemptions.

Third, this ruling is particularly significant and troubling in the kind of religious exemption it accords to corporations. The ruling confers on corporations the right to trump and effectively extinguish the rights of its employees. This is a very significant ruling, effectively exalting the rights of corporations over the individuals who work there. The ruling gives Hobby Lobby the power to take away from its employees—who have deeply held convictions of their own—the rights the Affordable Care Act insisted on to protect access to the full range of contraceptives. We can get into this later on, but the ruling's broad sweep opens the floodgates to a host of new claims for religious exemptions under RFRA.

Finally, let me highlight two aspects of the decision that are particularly striking and make the ruling such a sweeping one. First, Justice Alito's opinion takes a very broad view of the rights of corporations, making a number of points Ilya has been making through these debates. The linchpin of Justice Alito's reasoning is that a corporation is "simply a form of organization used by human beings to achieve desired ends" and that corporations like Hobby Lobby have rights, including religious free exercise rights, in order to protect the "liberty of the humans who own and control" the companies. This is broad reasoning that lays the basis for the Roberts Court to continue adding to the rights that corporations possess. Second, the majority interprets RFRA not simply as

DOI: 10.1057/9781137479709.0007

restoring pre-*Smith* law but as fundamentally changing it. The Court read RFRA as mandating a wider swath of religious exemptions than the Supreme Court ever did in its pre-*Smith* opinions construing the First Amendment's free exercise guarantee.[6] In Alito's hands, RFRA was designed "to effect a complete separation from First Amendment caselaw,"[7] creating a new body of law mandating a host of religious exemptions, including to corporations.

Rosen: Great, well let's indeed wait for a moment to talk about the kind of claims that could be opened but Ilya, David, like Justice Ginsburg, said this is a big deal because this is the first time that a corporations' religious liberty interests have been recognized and Justice Ginsburg distinguished the one other case involving Jewish merchants (*Braunfeld*) who sought exemptions from Sabbath laws on the grounds that those were sole proprietorships. They were individuals as opposed to closely held corporations. Have you been persuaded by Justice Ginsburg's objection?

Shapiro: No, and that's because of the way that RFRA is set up. It's meant to produce case-by-case adjudication. It's not that someone throws up a religious objection to some law and they win automatically. Some states have been trying to pass mini-RFRAs that are as broad as that and those have either not gone very far or have been struck down, but this is not that.

It's kind of a funny discussion we're having here. Typically, after a closely divided, controversial, high-profile Supreme Court decision, the winning side tries to trumpet how broad an opinion it is, showing that this will be a sea change in the law affecting the way that American life goes forward, while the losers try to minimize the loss. Here we have the reverse. That is, I think, a product of how both sides have really seen the case all along. For example, David talked about how the rights of employees, or of women, to access contraceptives are being subverted or extinguished. That's not happening at all. Women, whether they're employed by Hobby Lobby or anybody else, have the right to access whatever legal contraceptive or other product they want. This is not a case where even the employer is saying, "Aha! People who use or spend their money on these types of products, we will not employ them. If we find out about you using them, we'll fire you!" That would be a different case. It might be a closer case. It might come out the same way. It might be different. But that's a different case.

DOI: 10.1057/9781137479709.0007

Here, it's about the mandate on the employer. And the point about corporate rights is that corporate rights don't exist in a vacuum. The Dictionary Act, which applies to RFRA, like many statutes, defines "person" very broadly and there is a reason that "person" is defined broadly to include a whole host of entities, not just corporations or for-profits or businesses, but a whole host of entities. Why? To enable commerce, to facilitate contractual relationships, and to protect the rights, constitutional and otherwise, of the people associated with those groups, in this case, the owners, managers, and founders of closely held corporations. I think this leads to greater liberty—religious liberty certainly—than we had before. And the Court has said that it'll evaluate future religious objections on a case-by-case basis.

The Court noted that, for example, *United States v. Lee*, which David and I have talked about in the past, would have to come out the same way were it brought today. That case involved a religious objection to generalized payments of Social Security taxes. Justice Alito says, correctly, that to allow that religious exemption to triumph would result in chaos, with everyone objecting to lots of different things that they're supposed to pay to the government. This is a different type of case and RFRA is designed that way. This isn't the Court trying to minimize what they're doing. This is the nature of this particular statute. By the way, if popular opinion is so against this ruling, Congress can change RFRA or to repeal it—but it's an odd situation where this unanimously popular law from 20 years ago is all of a sudden part of a postmodern "war on women."

Rosen: David, there were a number of interesting points in Justice Alito's opinion. First he says because the Obama administration conceded that non-profit corporations could be considered persons, this concession dispatches any idea that for-profit corporations aren't covered because there is no dictionary definition of the phrase "corporations" that could include non-profits but not for-profits. So are you persuaded by that distinction?

Gans: No, I am not persuaded and the reason goes back to the unbroken history from the Founding until *Hobby Lobby* of treating religious organizations differently from commercial enterprises when it comes to religious free exercise rights. As Justice Ginsburg emphasized in her dissenting opinion, there has always been a fundamental difference between secular, for-profit corporations, organized to make running a business more profitable, and churches and other religious bodies, organized for the purpose of engaging in religious exercise. Religious groups have long been protected by the constitutional guarantee of free exercise and have long accorded religious exemptions. That's never been true of secular, for-profit corporations such as Hobby Lobby. Justice Alito's opinion ignores this longstanding, basic difference.

If you look back at the Court's religious free exercise precedents over the last two centuries, there have been a number of cases in which business owners have argued that the Free Exercise Clause demanded a religious exemption from general business regulation. Those have always been rejected. And, until *Hobby Lobby*, no court had held that a business corporation possessed religious free exercise rights and was entitled to a religious exemption from laws protecting the rights of the corporation's employees. Justice Alito's opinion effectively rewrites free exercise law, according secular, for-profit corporations religious exemptions previously limited to churches and other religious bodies.

In doing so, Justice Alito's opinion struck a severe blow to the rights of employees. A church or other religious group is designed to be a community of believers, united by their religious faith and devoted to spreading a commonly-held religious message. The same is not true of a secular business. Hobby Lobby is not a religious group. It's not organized that way and does not hire its employees based on religion. In affording Hobby Lobby a religious exemption, the Court gave secular businesses a right to impose their religious views on their employees and extinguish their rights.

Ilya disagrees, and he emphasizes that Justice Alito's ruling merely exempts a business from having to pay for contraceptives to which the owners are religious opposed. He observes that the *Hobby Lobby* ruling does not specifically countenance firing employees who use their own money to purchase contraceptives. That's a different issue, he says, one the Court does not decide. That's true but irrelevant.

The Affordable Care Act (ACA) sought to guarantee to employees access to the full range of FDA-approved contraceptives, recognizing that, without insurance coverage, women would not have access to the most effective forms of contraceptives, such as the IUD. The whole point of the Affordable Care Act in this area is that historically insurance companies wouldn't cover contraceptives for women on the same basis as prescription coverage for men. Accordingly, the ACA required employers' group

DOI: 10.1057/9781137479709.0007

health plans to cover the full range of FDA-approved contraceptives, creating a federal right to such coverage to protect women's health and safeguard their reproductive freedom. The Court's ruling allows Hobby Lobby's owners to impose their religious beliefs on their employees and extinguish the rights the ACA meant to secure. This result turns religious liberty on its head, giving employers a tremendous power over their employees. Employees should not have to check their personal liberty and human dignity at the workplace door. I think Justice Ginsburg really kind of hit the nail on the head when she wrote, that "[y]our right to swing your arms ends just where the other man's nose begins."[8] Her point was that, even under the broad scope we give to fundamental rights, such as free speech and free exercise of religion, once you step on someone else's rights, your own fundamental rights end. I think the Court missed that lesson.

Rosen: Yes, Justice Ginsburg did quote Zechariah Chafee and invoked John Stuart Mill's harm principle. On the other hand, Justice Alito responded with a moral quotation of his own, which led to one of the most philosophically sophisticated footnotes I've seen in a Supreme Court decision recently. He said, the question isn't whether the owners of these corporations are imposing their religious beliefs on their employees? The question is the appropriate "circumstances under which it is wrong for a person to perform an act that's innocent in itself, but that has the effect of enabling or facilitating the commission of an immoral act by another." And, then, we have footnote 34, citing David Oderberg's *The Ethics of Cooperation* and a series of other extremely substantial tones of moral philosophy.[10] Ilya, are you persuaded by Justice Alito's counter to John Stuart Mill and his notion that it's not appropriate for the government to be making decisions about what kind of moral beliefs are reasonable in these circumstances?

Shapiro: Well, clearly, Justice Alito or one of the other justices has a clerk who majored in philosophy or has some sort of graduate degree because, indeed, that's a very deep analysis in the footnote you mentioned. I'm generally persuaded by Justice Alito's opinion, but the broader point is: it's the government that's imposing a mandate here. It's not a question of what the employer is or isn't doing to its employees. It's a question of what is the government requiring of people, and whether that treatment can be justified under this statutory scheme—the Religious Freedom Restoration Act—that tells courts how they are to evaluate claims for

DOI: 10.1057/9781137479709.0007

religious exemptions. And, on that basis, the whole question of corporate rights is a distraction. It isn't really what this case is all about.

It doesn't really matter—as I said in the amicus brief that Cato filed in the case—how lawyers dress-up the claim about *who* has the right or the freedom of religious exercise, whether it's the corporation or the individuals that make it up. The key instead is the burden that the government imposes on that exercise; the burden that's being evaluated under the RFRA rubric is a burden on individual human beings who don't check their religious beliefs at church or at home. And so, just as an individual is allowed to conduct herself however she wants until that proverbial fist hits somebody else's nose, she can run her business in a host of ways unless the government can prove that it has a compelling interest to trump that freedom—and the means it uses to advance that interest is basically the only way it can do so.

I mean, in a certain sense, David and I are like two ships passing in the night. I'm arguing from the statutory text of RFRA, while David is talking about the First Amendment and third-party effects. I don't know if that means David disagrees with the Court's evaluation of the narrowly tailored requirement because that's how this case was ultimately resolved. At the end of the day, Hobby Lobby won this case because the government could, for example, set up public clinics, provide other types of subsidies for employees, work with insurers to develop other methods of providing free access to these contraceptives. They've put in so-called accommodations for non-profit groups. These are being challenged on another basis by some of these non-profits, but they may well satisfy Hobby Lobby and Conestoga, the plaintiffs here. So, again, this is in some manner a technical, but simple, case because if you apply RFRA and you understand that RFRA deals with individual rights that are being burdened, you just look at whether the government had alternatives to burdening those rights to achieve the same goal. The result can't be anything other than what Justice Alito stated.

Rosen: So, David, that sounds rather glamorous, but are you two ships passing in the night? Ilya says you're just disagreeing about the application of the least-restrictive means test. Justice Ginsburg gets into this debate with Justice Alito as well. Justice Alito says let "the government pay." He argues that the most straightforward alternative would indeed be for the government to assume the cost of providing contraceptives to any women who are unable to obtain them from religiously objecting

DOI: 10.1057/9781137479709.0007

employers. Justice Ginsburg replies that the ACA requires coverage of the services in employers' existing policies and that impeding women's receipt of benefits by requiring them to take these new steps to learn about a government-funded program was not what Congress intended. Is that really the nub of the disagreement and not these broader First Amendment issues?

David H. Gans: Of course, at the end of the day, *Hobby Lobby* turns on the meaning and scope of RFRA. But what's notable is that the Court's conservative majority is moving the law to give new rights to corporations and to accord them a wide swathe of religious exemptions that have no precedent in any prior decision of the Court. Ilya's argument is that the government lost because it could have paid directly for contraceptive coverage—effectively moving the ACA in the direction of a single-payer system—but the Court's pre-*Smith* free exercise law is directly to the contrary. The same could have been said in *Lee*—the government could have covered the costs of the Social Security taxes required of Amish employers—but the Court held that sort of exemption was not required by free exercise principles (even though the government already had provided an exemption to self-employed Amish). Rather, the Court unanimously ruled that the Free Exercise Clause did not require an exemption that would "impose the employer's religious faith on the employees."[11] Not one member of the *Lee* Court thought that principles of religious liberty required giving business owners such tremendous power over their employees.

Ilya also mentions that the government could have offered Hobby Lobby and other secular, for-profit employers the accommodation given to religiously affiliated non-profit organizations. But the Court leaves open the question whether that accommodation itself violates RFRA.[12] So, it is really difficult to treat that accommodation as a suitable alternative. In any event, as Justice Ginsburg pointed out in dissent, religious employers have long been given religious accommodations, which have "never been accorded to commercial enterprises comprising employees of diverse faiths."[13]

The Court's opinion in *Hobby Lobby* is momentous, breaking sharply from *Lee* and other past cases and mandating religious exemptions in cases in which the Court had rejected them. In so doing, the Roberts Court's conservative majority has created a new law of religion, one that tilts sharply in favor of corporations. That, I think, explains the very

DOI: 10.1057/9781137479709.0007

sharp disagreements between Justice Alito, writing for the majority, and Justice Ginsburg, in dissent. We have two very different views in these opinions about the rights of corporations.

Three critical features, together, make the *Hobby Lobby* ruling a very far reaching one. First, its central holding strongly suggests that all corporations—not merely those that are closely held—are entitled to demand religious exemptions from generally applicable business regulation. Despite claims to narrowness, the opinion's reasoning is that a corporation is simply the artificial embodiment of its owners and shareholders, and must have the same free exercise rights as individuals. That's a sweeping pronouncement. Second, it announced a very loose version of what constitutes a "substantial burden" triggering strict scrutiny, deferring to the claims of religious objectors that a law substantially burdens religious exercise. This water-downed test threatens to open the door for major portions the U.S. code to be subject to strict scrutiny. Third, the opinion applies a particular strict version of the "least restrictive alternative test"—one of the harshest in constitutional law—making it very difficult for the government to defeat claims for religious exemptions, even when those exemptions extinguish the rights of employees.

Taken together, these features open the floodgates to a lot of new claims for religious exemptions down the road, on matters ranging from antidiscrimination law to other medical procedures such as blood transfusions or vaccinations. In this respect, *Hobby Lobby* represents a substantial break from how courts have handled this in the past. There is really no body of law that offers the kind and scope of religious accommodations that Justice Alito describes. This is a huge development that, for the first time in American history, grants free exercise rights to corporations and exalts corporations over individuals, allowing corporate CEOs to impose their religious beliefs on their employees and extinguish their federal rights. Now, we'll see down the road how far this goes. But I think it's extremely important and troubling ruling.

It may well turn out that, as some have predicted, "religious exemptions are in fact rarely loosed and thereafter quite readily cabined."[14] It may be that Justice Kennedy, whose concurring opinion suggests he may read the case more narrowly than other members of the majority, will be reluctant to extend the majority's reasoning to create new religious exemptions. All of that is possible. But what we are already seeing in the aftermath of the ruling are new claims for religious exemptions.

DOI: 10.1057/9781137479709.0007

Conservative groups have criticized President Obama's executive order forbidding government contractors from engaging in discrimination on account of sexual orientation, arguing that "[p]eople with deeply held convictions regarding the morality of certain types of sexual behavior should not be bound by the dictates of President Obama's agenda."[15] I think we will continue to see new claims of this sort, seeking to expand and build off Justice Alito's opinion in *Hobby Lobby*.

If we look to the Dictionary Act's definition of person—on which Ilya and the Court rely—what is critical is context. When RFRA was passed, no court had ever announced that secular, for-profit corporations were entitled to religious free exercise rights or accorded them religious exemptions from laws protecting the rights of their employees. Now in one fell swoop, the Court has used RFRA to do both, creating a revolution in corporate free exercise rights and providing religious exemptions without any basis in precedent. This is an opinion that does violence to RFRA's goal of restoring protections for religious liberty taken away in the *Smith* case. So while this was not a constitutional ruling—and thus easier to correct than a ruling interpreting the Free Exercise Clause—it is still an extremely significant decision that doubles down on corporate personhood and uses it to undercut the rights of living Americans in a way that is very harmful.

Rosen: Well Ilya, David is continuing your aquatic analogies. You talked about ships passing in the night, and he says that the Court has opened the floodgates—and Justice Ginsburg agrees. She creates a whole series of possibilities. She says, "Would the exemption the Court holds RFRA demands for employers with religiously grounded objections to the use of certain contraceptives extend to employers with religiously grounded objections to blood transfusions (Jehovah's Witnesses); antidepressants (Scientologists); medications derived from pigs, including anesthesia, intravenous fluids, and pills coated with gelatin (certain Muslims, Jews, and Hindus); and vaccinations (Christian Scientists)" and so forth.[16] Is this parade of horribles or open floodgates fair or not?

Shapiro: That's a fair question, but Justice Alito's opinion for the majority and Justice Kennedy's concurring opinion don't shy away from addressing the parade of horribles. They mention them and say that those will be other cases, which can be considered on their own merits when they come before the courts.[17] That's the nature of the system of judicial review under RFRA; it tells courts to consider claims on a case-by-case basis, balancing burdens and interests and evaluating the narrowness of the means. And certain types of claims are non-starters: a company can't engage in racial discrimination cloaked as religious exercise, for example.[18]

Further, it's the government here that manufactured this challenge, that manufactured this values conflict. I wish Congress would pass the Economic Freedom Restoration Act, the Property Freedom Restoration Act, the Speech Freedom Restoration Act—all laws that double down on the Constitution, that raise the level of legal protection for fundamental rights. That would show that we Americans are serious about protecting our liberty.[19]

Here, we just happen to be dealing with the government's violation of religious liberties, not of corporate religious liberties. Corporate personhood is immaterial—as it is to the quote from Justice Ginsburg that you just used. It would be immaterial, as Justice Alito describes, if the owners of Hobby Lobby pursued their business in the form of a limited liability company or a partnership or a sole proprietorship or any other way. It's not the corporate form that dictates how much or little liberty they have. After all, it's not Oklahoma—where Hobby Lobby is incorporated—that's objecting about some misuse of the corporate structure. Instead, this is about individual rights being violated. And in some future case, if some future employer doesn't want to cover, say, blood transfusions, then the Court will evaluate whether, indeed, a mandate to cover blood transfusions is a substantial burden on that belief. Even in the case of Jehovah's Witnesses, it may not be; they might only object to transfusions for themselves, not those of other faiths. But if it were, then the question would be whether it's a compelling state interest for the government nevertheless to insist on it and is there some other way to accomplish that goal without mandating it? Who would win that one depends, like this case, on whether the government's interest in universal "free" blood transfusions is compelling and whether that goal can be achieved in some way other than an employer mandate. That's not a slam dunk by any means, but that controversy is another example of the problems that government creates when it imposes mandates. What would be an easy case—and I hope David would agree, even if Justice Ginsburg doesn't use this example—would be a follower of an ancient Aztec religion who sought an exemption from criminal laws so he could practice human sacrifice. This is the rubric and analysis required by RFRA, and we can debate how RFRA should apply in that particular case.

DOI: 10.1057/9781137479709.0007

Again, *Hobby Lobby* is not about expanding corporate rights other than in recognizing, under the Dictionary Act and under RFRA, as David correctly identified, that corporations and other non-human entities are legal persons. Because Congress didn't limit the definition of "person," they are. I think that's hard to dispute. So, the parade of horribles has to be left for another day. If all of a sudden we have religious objectors coming out of the woodwork to object to everything that the government does—though they've had 20 years to do so!—then Congress might reconsider the scope of RFRA. Or Congress might reconsider what the government itself is doing. Ultimately, this comes down to a relationship between the government and the governed and what kind of burdens the government can put on people.

Rosen: Okay gentlemen, time for closing arguments. David, why should Americans care about this case? Is it part of broader trend toward recognizing the First Amendment rights of corporations? What do you think the broader significance of this case will be?

Gans: I certainly think it is part of a broader trend. Across a wide range of First Amendment doctrines, we are seeing the Roberts Court make the First Amendment's guarantees of freedom of speech and free exercise of religion into a sword to free corporations and other powerful interests from government regulation. We've seen that in campaign finance cases, like *Citizens United v. FEC*, and commercial speech cases, like *Sorrell v. IMS Health Inc.*,[20] which made it easier for corporations to strike down laws regulating advertising and other forms of commercial speech. The ruling in *Hobby Lobby* opens up an entirely new avenue for corporations to attack government regulation, giving corporations for the first time in history the power to demand religious exemptions from laws protecting the rights of their employees.[21]

Notably, in *Hobby Lobby*, the Roberts Court is doing much more in the name of RFRA than it could in the name of the First Amendment, invoking RFRA to create a new body of free exercise that tilts sharply in favor of corporations. Going forward, this makes RFRA into a potentially powerful tool for new religious exemptions for corporations.

I disagree that this isn't about creating new rights for corporations. The Court allows Hobby Lobby to have its cake and eat it too, claiming all the special privileges given to corporations as well as fundamental rights designed to protect freedom of conscience and human dignity. The

Court allows the Greens to hide behind the corporate veil when sued, while also claiming fundamental, personal rights as corporate owners. The result is a massive expansion in the rights of and power of corporations. It is undeniable that this is the first case in more than two centuries to extend to corporations rights of religious exercise and accord them religious exemptions.

It creates a very dangerous precedent that threatens to undermine—not protect—religious liberty by exalting the rights of corporations over those individuals who employed there. Under Justice Alito's ruling, if you go to work for Hobby Lobby, your rights are subject to the whims of the owners and can be overridden if the owner insists that your rights conflict with the owner's religious view. That a huge and dangerous change in the law. It gives corporations new rights they never before possessed. For the reasons expressed by Justice Ginsburg, this is deeply incorrect ruling that has no basis in free exercise principles, precedent, or RFRA.

Rosen: Ilya, time for your closing argument. So what is the significance of the case and the debates over it?

Shapiro: The case is important for understanding what rights corporations have and why they have them. To summarize my basic point: it's not just empowering corporations and other collective entities just for their own sake; it's to protect the rights of the individuals that make them up, just like Bill de Blasio, the Mayor of New York, can't take over Rockefeller Center to put his office there without paying just compensation because the corporation that owns the real estate has Fifth Amendment rights. For similar reasons, the police can't go into the National Constitution Center or the Cato Institute—or Hobby Lobby for that matter—without a warrant or probable cause because those entities have Fourth Amendment rights to protect the individuals that make them up. It's the same thing here, and ultimately the ruling flows from the fact that the Greens—the owners, controllers, directors of these companies—have religious free exercise rights that must be respected. That's why the opinion speaks of closely held corporations. It would be hard to envision a Fortune 500 company with all the shareholders and everyone else aligned in the same way. Theoretically, it could happen, but it's extremely unlikely.

More broadly, this ruling properly limits the power of government to impose these incredible, unprecedented mandates and other types of Leviathan burdens on the citizenry as this administration has. That's

DOI: 10.1057/9781137479709.0007

why, ultimately, the Court has to make these calls, and adjudicate what, in its time, was the noncontroversial Religious Freedom Restoration Act, which was pushed by those religious zealots Ted Kennedy and Chuck Schumer.[22]

Rosen: Thank you so much, Ilya Shapiro and David Gans, for having consistently illuminated for our patrons, this most contentious and interesting of all constitutional cases this term. We're so grateful for your insights and we're so grateful for the listeners of the "We The People" constitutional podcast for having joined us for a blockbuster Supreme Court term. The Supreme Court is out now but the podcast, and our town halls, will continue.

Notes

1   This chapter is based on a National Constitution Center podcast recorded June 30, 2014, soon after the Supreme Court's ruling in the *Hobby Lobby* case.

2   *Burwell v. Hobby Lobby Stores, Inc.*, 134 S. Ct. 2751, 2774–75 (2014); *see also id.* at 2768 ("Corporations, 'separate and apart from' the human beings who own, run, and are employed by them, cannot do anything at all." (quoting *Conestoga Wood Specialties Corp. v. Sec'y HHS*, 724 F.3d 377, 385 (3d Cir. 2013)).

3   *Hobby Lobby*, 134 S. Ct. at 2782–83.

4   *Id.* at 2787 (Ginsburg, J., dissenting).

5   *Id.* at 2768.

6   See *id.* at 2784 n.43 (rejecting the government's reliance on *Lee* by observing that "*Lee* was a free exercise, not a RFRA, case" and that *Lee*'s reasoning "is squarely inconsistent with the plain meaning of RFRA").

7   *Id.* at 2762.

8   *Id.* at 2791 (Ginsburg, J., dissenting) (quoting Zechariah Chafee, *Freedom of Speech in War Time*, 32 Harv. L. Rev. 932, 957 (1919)).

9   *Id.* at 2778.

10   *Id.* at 2778 n.34.

11   *Lee*, 455 U.S. at 261.

12   *Hobby Lobby*, 134 S. Ct. at 2782 & n.39; *id.* at 2803 (Ginsburg, J., dissenting) ("Ultimately, the Court hedges on its proposal to align for-profit enterprises with non-profit religion-based organizations").

13   *Id.*

14   Ira Lupu, Hobby Lobby and the Dubious Enterprise of Religious Exemptions, at 60 (forthcoming *Harv. J. of Law & Gender* 2015), available at http://papers.ssrn.com/sol3/papers.cfm?abstract_id=2466571.

DOI: 10.1057/9781137479709.0007

15 *See* Family Research Council, Press Release, ENDA Executive Order Burdens
    Employers, Imposes on Free Speech, Constitutional Liberties (July 21, 2014),
    available at http://www.frc.org/pressrelease/enda-executive-order-burdens-
    employers-imposes-on-free-speech-constitutional-liberties.

16 *Hobby Lobby*, 134 S. Ct. at 2805 (Ginsburg, J., dissenting).

17 *Id.* at 2783 (Alito, J., for the Court) ("Our decision should not be understood
    to hold that an insurance-coverage mandate must necessarily fall if it
    conflicts with an employer's religious beliefs. Other coverage requirements,
    such as immunizations, may be supported by different interests (for example,
    the need to combat the spread of infectious diseases) and may involve
    different arguments about the least restrictive means of providing them.");
    id. at 2787 (Kennedy, J., concurring) ("As the Court explains, this existing
    model, designed precisely for this problem, might well suffice to distinguish
    the instant cases from many others in which it is more difficult and expensive
    to accommodate a governmental program to countless religious claims based
    on an alleged statutory right of free exercise.").

18 *Id.* at 2783 (Alito, J., for the Court) ("The Government has a compelling
    interest in providing an equal opportunity to participate in the workforce
    without regard to race, and prohibitions on racial discrimination are
    precisely tailored to achieve that critical goal.").

19 It gives me (Ilya) great pride to say "*we* Americans" because I was naturalized
    10 days before the Supreme Court ruled in this case.

20 131 S. Ct. 2653 (2011).

21 For fuller discussion, see David H. Gans, The Roberts Court Thinks
    Corporations Have More Rights Than You, *The New Republic* (June 30, 2014),
    available at http://www.newrepublic.com/article/118493/john-roberts-first-
    amendment-revolution-corporations.

22 For a fuller discussion, see Ilya Shapiro, Hobby Lobby: Government Can't
    Violate Religious Liberties Willy Nilly, *The Federalist* (July 1, 2014), http://
    thefederalist.com/2014/07/01/hobby-lobby-government-cant-violate-
    religious-liberties-willy-nilly/.

DOI: 10.1057/9781137479709.0007

Conclusion

Abstract: *Both authors offer concluding thoughts on corporate rights, religious liberties, RFRA, and the future of law and politics in this area.*

Keywords: corporate rights; health care; individual rights; values

Gans, David H., and Ilya Shapiro. *Religious Liberties for Corporations?: Hobby Lobby, the Affordable Care Act, and the Constitution.* New York: Palgrave Macmillan, 2014. DOI: 10.1057/9781137479709.0008.

David H. Gans: At the Founding, the Framers never mentioned corporations in the Constitution, fearful that these artificial entities would become all powerful. Nevertheless, Chief Justice Roberts, in just under a decade, has moved the Supreme Court sharply to the right, inventing new rights for corporations and rewriting our fundamental constitutional principles. In rulings like *Citizens United*, *Hobby Lobby*, and others, Roberts and his conservative colleagues are jettisoning critical aspects of our Constitution's text and history, ignoring the Founders' wisdom that corporations were not part of "We the People" and that extending equal rights to corporations would prove harmful to the American people.

The linchpin of these Roberts Court rulings is that corporations, like individuals, deserve fundamental constitutional rights because corporations are associations of people. But these rulings go much further, giving corporations rights that no individuals possess. *Citizens United* held that corporations may use the special privileges they alone possess—and which make them uniquely powerful and wealthy—to spend unlimited sums of money to elect candidates do their bidding. *Hobby Lobby* gives the owners of closed, secular for-profit corporations—businesses that by some estimates employ half the nation's workforce—the power to impose their own religious beliefs on their employees and deny them important federal rights. In these rulings and others, the Roberts Court is rewriting the basic rules of our system of government, giving corporations more rights than individuals.

Ilya Shapiro: Despite all the hue and cry, *Hobby Lobby* was a simple case involving two straightforward issues. First, everyone agrees that corporations have *some* rights, so the battle is always over the scope of those rights. Here, the Court easily found that RFRA's definition of "person" includes corporations. In many circumstances, corporations—for-profit or not; that distinction is irrelevant to this analysis—may not have constitutional or statutory rights. But at least where the government forces the owners of closely held corporations to "choose" between violating their religious beliefs and paying exorbitant fines, there's a problem.

Second, RFRA's framework is clear: if a government action substantially burdens religious exercise, courts evaluate whether it nevertheless pursues a compelling interest in the least-burdensome way possible. Here, the government didn't even attempt to show that other means weren't feasible—probably because it couldn't—so it failed to carry its statutory

DOI: 10.1057/9781137479709.0008

burden. Perhaps we should change RFRA, but under its current language the result is obvious.

Moreover, while our focus here has been the intersection of corporate rights and religious liberties, there's a bigger issue. *Hobby Lobby* is just the latest example of the difficulties inherent in turning healthcare—or our economy more broadly—over to the government. When something is socialized or treated as a public utility, values clash as people fight for every "carve-out" of liberty.[1] Those who supported Hobby Lobby here are rightly concerned that people are being forced to do what their consciences prohibit. But that all comes with the collectivized territory.

Note

1 *See* Roger Pilon, Will the GOP Win the Birth Control Fight?, *The Arena* (February 9, 2012), available at http://www.politico.com/arena/perm/ Roger_Pilon_2512A673-DCE4-4698-959D-DD00F212A676.html.

DOI: 10.1057/9781137479709.0008

Bibliography

Books and Articles

Akhil Reed Amar, *The Bill of Rights: Creation and Reconstruction* (1998), Yale UP, New Haven.

William Blackstone, *Commentaries on the Law of England* (1768), Clarendon Press, Oxford.

J. Cox and T. Hazen, *Treatise of the Law of Corporations* (3d ed. 2010), Aspen Publishers, Aspen.

Daniel Crane, Antitrust Antifederalism, 96 *Cal. L. Rev.* 1 (2008).

W. Fletcher, *Cyclopedia of the Law of Corporations* (rev. ed. 2010), Clark Boardman Callaghan, New York.

David H. Gans, Discrimination, Inc. (February 28, 2014) (available at http://blog.constitutioncenter.org/2014/02/discrimination-inc/).

David H. Gans, The Roberts Court Thinks Corporations Have More Rights Than You, *The New Republic* (June 30, 2014) (available at http://www.newrepublic.com/article/118493/john-roberts-first-amendment-revolution-corporations).

David H. Gans and Douglas T. Kendall, A Capitalist Joker: The Strange Origins, Disturbing Past, and Uncertain Future of Corporate Personhood in American Law (2010) (available at http://theusconstitution.org/think-tank/narrative/capitalist-joker-corporations-corporate-personhood-and-constitution).

DOI: 10.1057/9781137479709.0009

Douglas Laycock, Towards a General Theory of the Religion Clauses: The Case of Church Labor Relations and the Right to Church Autonomy, 81 *Colum. L. Rev.* 1373 (1981).

John Locke, a Letter Concerning Toleration (1689) (James H. Tully Ed., 1983), Hackett Publishing, Indianapolis.

Ira Lupu, Hobby Lobby and the Dubious Enterprise of Religious Exemptions (forthcoming *Harv. J. of Law & Gender*, 2015) (available at http://papers.ssrn.com/sol3/papers.cfm?abstract_id=2466571).

James Madison, Memorial and Remonstrance against Religious Assessments, *in* 2 *The Writings of James Madison* (G. Hunt Ed., 1901), Madison.

Michael W. McConnell, The Origins and Historical Understanding of Free Exercise of Religion, 103 *Harv. L. Rev.* 1409 (1990).

Roger Pilon, Will the GOP Win the Birth Control Fight?, *The Arena* (February 9, 2012) (available at http://www.politico.com/arena/perm/ Roger_Pilon_2512A673-DCE4-4698-959D-DD00F212A676.html).

James E. Ryan, Note, Smith and the Religious Freedom Restoration Act: An Iconoclastic Assessment, 78 *Va. L. Rev.* 1407 (1992).

Ilya Shapiro, *For Marriage Equality, Religious Liberty, and Freedom of Association*, Cato at Liberty (February 26, 2014) (available at http:// www.cato.org/blog/marriage-equality-religious-liberty-freedom-association).

Ilya Shapiro, *Hobby Lobby: Government Can't Violate Religious Liberties Willy Nilly*, the Federalist (July 1, 2014) (available at http:// thefederalist.com/2014/07/01/hobby-lobby-government-cant-violate-religious-liberties-willy-nilly/).

Ilya Shapiro and Caitlin W. McCarthy, So What If Corporations Aren't People, 44 *John Marshall L. Rev.* 701 (2011).

William Stuntz, The Substantive Origins of Criminal Procedure, 105 *Yale L. J.* 363, 411–12 (1995).

Eugene Volokh, *Constitutional Rights and Corporations*, The Volokh Conspiracy (September 22, 2009, 12:44 PM) (available at http://volokh.com/posts/1253637850.shtml).

Eugene Volokh, Sebelius V. Hobby Lobby: *Corporate Rights and Religious Liberties* (2014), Cato Institute, Washington.

Adam Winkler, Corporations and the First Amendment: Examining the Health of Democracy: Corporate Personhood and the Rights of Corporate Speech, 30 *Seattle L. Rev.* 863 (2007).

DOI: 10.1057/9781137479709.0009

Cases

Adams v. Commissioner of Internal Revenue, 170 F.3d 173, 178 (3d Cir. 1999).

Bank of Augusta v. Earle, 38 U.S. (13 Pet.) 519 (1839).

Braswell v. United States, 487 U.S. 99, 119 (1988).

Braunfeld v. Brown, 366 U.S. 599 (1961).

Burwell v. Hobby Lobby Stores, Inc., 2014 WL 2921709 (2014).

Cedric Kushner Promotions, Ltd. v. King, 533 U.S. 158, 163 (2001).

Chicago B. & Q. R. Co. v. City of Chicago, 166 U.S. 226 (1897).

Citizens United v. FEC, 558 U.S. 310 (2010).

City of Boerne v. Flores, 521 U.S. 507 (1997).

Conestoga Wood Specialties Corp. v. Sec'y of the U.S. Dep't of Health & Human Servs., 724 F.3d 377 (3d Cir. 2013).

Domino's Pizza, Inc. v. McDonald, 546 U.S. 470 (2006).

Employment Division v. Smith, 494 U.S. 872 (1990).

FCC v. AT & T, Inc., 131 S. Ct. 1177 (2011).

First National Bank of Boston v. Bellotti, 435 U.S. 765 (1978).

Frazee v. Illinois Dep't of Emp. Sec., 489 U.S. 829 (1989).

Gilardi v. U.S. Dep't of Health & Human Servs., 733 F.3d 1208 (D.C. Cir. 2013).

Gloucester Ferry Co. v. Pennsylvania, 114 U.S. 196 (1885).

Gulf, C. & S.F. Ry. Co. v. Ellis, 165 U.S. 150 (1897).

Hobbie v. Unemployment Appeals Comm'n, 480 U.S. 136 (1987).

Hobby Lobby Stores, Inc. v. Sebelius, 723 F.3d 1114 (10th Cir. 2013) (en banc).

Hosanna-Tabor Evangelical Lutheran Church and School v. EEOC, 132 S. Ct. 694 (2012).

Jacobson v. Massachusetts, 197 U.S. 11 (1905).

Korte v. Sebelius, 735 F.3d 654 (7th Cir. 2013).

Louisville, Cincinnati & Charleston R. Co. v. Letson, 43 U.S. (2 How.) 397 (1844).

Marshall v. Barlow's Inc., 436 U.S. 307 (1978).

McGowan v. Maryland, 366 U.S. 420 (1960).

Nat'l Fed'n of Independent Business v. Sebelius, 132 S. Ct. 256 (2012).

Prince v. Massachusetts, 321 U.S. 158 (1944).

Roberts v. United States Jaycees, 468 U.S. 609 (1984).

Sherbert v. Verner, 374 U.S. 398 (1963).

Thomas v. Review Bd. of the Indiana Emp. Sec. Div., 450 U.S. 707 (1981).

DOI: 10.1057/9781137479709.0009

Trustees of Dartmouth College v. Woodward, 17 U.S. (4 Wheat.) 518 (1819).

United States v. Lee, 455 U.S. 282 (1982).

United States v. Morton Salt Co., 338 U.S. 632 (1950).

United States v. White, 322 U.S. 694 (1944).

Western Turf Ass'n v. Greenberg, 204 U.S. 359 (1907).

DOI: 10.1057/9781137479709.0009

Index

DOI: 10.1057/9781137479709.0010

CPSIA information can be obtained at www.ICGtesting.com
Printed in the USA
LVOW06*1759031214

416972LV00006B/27/P